FORTRAN
GETTING STARTED

WILLIAM S. DAVIS   MIAMI UNIVERSITY

D1224438

▲▼ ADDISON-WESLEY PUBLISHING COMPANY

Reading, Massachusetts □ Menlo Park, California
London □ Amsterdam □ Don Mills, Ontario □ Sydney

to Jack

Library of Congress Cataloging in Publication Data

Davis, William S., 1943-
    FORTRAN, getting started.

    1. FORTRAN (Computer program language)
I. Title.
QA76.73.F25D386   001.64'24   81- 893
ISBN 0-201-03104-3   AACR2

Reproduced by Addison-Wesley from camera-ready copy approved by the author.

ISBN 0-201-03104-3
    DEFGHIJ- AL- 89876543

Preface

The fact that you are reading this book indicates that you would like to learn to write computer programs. Perhaps you envision a professional career. You may need a tool to support your research. Your major department may require a programming course. Do you own a personal computer? If so, playing games designed by someone else may be losing its appeal. It could be that you are just curious, and want to learn more about these machines. The reasons are many.

If you want to learn how to program, you must begin somewhere. The intent of this book is simple: to help you get started. It is likely that the most difficult program you will ever write will be your very first one. Our objective is to guide you step-by-step through your first few programs until you are "over the hump" and feel comfortable with the machine.

There is an axiom in the computer field: The only way to learn to program *is* to program. We subscribe to that axiom. Once you have mastered the basics, the only way to improve your skill will be to write more programs. That is up to you.

But what does "to program" mean? Beginners often assume that programming is simply writing instructions in a programming language. A program is a series of instructions much as a novel is a series of sentences; syntax, spelling, and grammer are important, but there is more to the novel—and the program! The beginner who misses this essential point often becomes so bogged down in rules and syntax, that nothing is accomplished. The student knows how to write a valid instruction, but does not know what instruction to write next.

A program *is* a series of instructions. More accurately, it's a series of instructions designed to tell the computer how to perform some function, such as how to compute an average, or how to compute payroll, or how to sort data into sequence. The computer has no intelligence of its own. The programmer supplies that intelligence by telling the computer *exactly* (and we do mean exactly) what do do. Before the programmer can tell the computer how to solve a problem, he or she must know how to solve that problem. The first step in the program development process is therefore a logical one: solve the problem, using such tools as intelligence, logic, mathematics, and common sense. Only when the problem has been solved should the programmer begin the largely mechanical process of translating that solution into a programming language.

In writing a program, the programmer must be able to answer two questions:

1. What instruction should I code next?

2. How do I code that instruction?

To answer the first question requires logic. The answer to the second question is more mechanical. Specific syntax and punctuation rules must be followed—they can be looked up in a reference manual. Practice is the key. *Anyone* can, given enough time, learn the rules of a programming language.

Logic is different. Logic *(What instruction do I code next?)* requires thought and planning. It is a mental process. It is easy to see what the person who is writing code is doing. Logic and planning are not so obvious or concrete. Professional programmers, of course, understand the dual nature of the programming task. A few beginners seem to grasp this idea intuitively. Many do not. Without a plan to provide a context, programming seems an almost magical art—try something and see if it works. Discouraged, many quit before they actually begin. Usually, the problem is not a lack of aptitude or ability; often, the beginner has simply not grasped what "to program" means.

And so, we return to our objective: helping you get started. We begin by developing a solution to a problem, without reference to any language. In Chapter 2, this solution is translated into FORTRAN and submitted to the computer, with each step clearly described. As your skill (and confidence) increases, you should have little trouble with the more complex problems that are solved and coded in subsequent chapters.

FORTRAN was the first of the compiler languages. Among those who use the computer as an aid to scientific computation, it remains perhaps the most popular. One of the reasons for FORTRAN's continuing popularity is the fact that the language has been standardized—a FORTRAN program written for computer "A" looks much like a FORTRAN program written for computer "B". Most existing FORTRAN compilers follow the American National Standards Institute's (ANSI) 1966 standards. Recently, a new, updated version, FORTRAN 77, was established. Gradually, the various computer manufacturers are modifying their compilers to comform to this new standard. The programs in this text are written to the FORTRAN 77 standard. They were tested under WATFIV-S, a popular academic compiler with extensions that support most FORTRAN 77 features.

As this book is written, few FORTRAN 77 compilers are available. Why, then, should students be trained on FORTRAN 77? The student is a potential *future* programmer. FORTRAN 77 *is* the FORTRAN of the future.

Please note that it is not our intent to cover every feature of FORTRAN 77. Our goal is to help you get started. Ideally, after reading this book and writing a few programs, you will be able to read the FORTRAN reference manual and discover new features for yourself. If so, we will have achieved our objective.

WSD

Oxford, Ohio

Contents

Defining
and Planning
a Problem Solution

1

OVERVIEW

In this chapter, we will follow, step-by-step, the process of developing a solution to a program suitable for submitting to a computer. The problem we've chosen is very general: computing an average. We'll begin by carefully defining the problem to be solved. Next, we'll structure a human-level solution, using such generally accepted and understood everyday tools as a pocket calculator and a counter. Having specified a fairly complete human-level solution, we'll briefly discuss a few elementary computer concepts and then restructure our solution to fit the requirements of these machines, developing a flowchart and a description of the data to be processed. Once these tasks have been completed, we'll be ready to begin coding the program in FORTRAN.

A CAUTIONARY NOTE BEFORE WE BEGIN

Computers are fascinating machines. But they are just machines, capable of doing nothing without detailed instructions provided by some human being. Because you are reading this book, you are probably interested in learning how to write these detailed sets of instructions, called programs. You must remember, however, that the computer can do *nothing* that you yourself do not know how to do. In other words, the responsibility for solving the problem is yours, and not the computer's. Yes, the computer is very accurate, but "accuracy" may not mean exactly what you think. Computers are considered accurate because the results they generate are highly predictable. If you tell a computer to add 2 and 2, it will invariably get 4. If the programmer didn't really mean to have the computer add 2 and 2, it will *still* get 4. The wrong instructions will produce the wrong answer with perfect "accuracy".

A computer is programmed in a programming language; the language we've chosen for this text is FORTRAN. Anyone can learn to write instructions in FORTRAN—it's just a matter of practice. There is, however, much more to programming. Before a problem solution can be coded in any language, there must be a problem solution. The primary purpose of this book is to show you how to develop such solutions. We'll be using a very methodical, structured approach, the top-down approach, to program development. As you begin to learn more about programming, the temptation will be to skip planning and careful preparation, and immediately begin coding a solution. Don't. As your skill increases, you will find yourself attempting more and more difficult problems, so the need for careful planning *never* disappears. *Think!* Then do.

DEFINING THE PROBLEM

Let's start with a very common problem: computing an average. Undoubtedly, you have computed your grade point average, your batting average, your freethrow percentage, or some other average. What does it mean to compute an average? If you had to perform this task, what would you do?

Your view of the problem is probably going to be shaded somewhat by your background. If you are a mathematician, your basic definition of this problem is simply

$$\bar{X} = \frac{\sum_{i=1}^{n} X_i}{n}$$

For many people, the mathematical definition isn't very useful. Perhaps, your view of the problem consists of the following two steps:

1. add together all the values you wish to average,

2. divide by the total number of values.

The result, in either case, will be an arithmetic average (or mean).

In technical terms, we have just defined an algorithm, a set of rules which, if followed precisely, will lead to a correct solution. Note that both the mathematical version and the English language version are valid algorithms; the use of mathematical conventions is *not* essential.

We now know, in very general terms, what has to be done. The question that remains is, "How do we do it?". Let's move along to the planning stage, where we will attempt to answer that question.

PLANNING A MANUAL SOLUTION

If you had to compute an average, precisely how would you go about it? We've already developed an algorithm; looking at that list of two steps, you might feel mildly insulted by the question. It seems obvious. Just

1. add all the values,

2. divide by the number of values.

It *is* obvious. You are, after all, a human being. Having stated the algorithm, you know how to solve the problem.

True. But that doesn't help us bring the problem solution down to the computer's level. We must be more precise. A useful technique for introducing this added detail is to set up a straw person. Assume that this person is unbelievably dense, and is capable of doing only what he or she is told to do. Instructions must be in the form of simple sentences—one verb. Each instruction must specify one and only one very specific action; this person literally cannot chew gum and walk at the same time. Now, tell this person how to compute an average. (You might even get your roommate to play the role.)

We might add a bit of structure to this technique by giving our straw person a pocket calculator (after all, everyone has a pocket calculator). We are now ready to begin instructing this imaginary individual as to exactly how to go about computing an arithmetic average.

What's wrong with simply saying, "Add all the numbers together"? How many numbers are there? If we assume there are 50 numbers, we are asking our straw person to do 50 things. The limit is 1! Our imaginary person can do only 1 thing at a time. We must be more precise.

Breaking this part of the problem into individual steps might produce the following list:

1. Enter the first number.

2. Push the ADD button.

3. Enter the second number.

4. Push the ADD button.

5. Enter the third number.

6. Push the ADD button, and so on.

The pattern should be obvious. Note that each instruction is a simple sentence telling the straw person to perform one and only one very specific function.

How many instructions would we need? If we wanted to find the average of 50 numbers, we would need 50 "Enters" and 50 "Adds". One thousand numbers would require 1000 sets of instructions. Defining a solution in this way would become tedious. Chances are, you would consider taking a shortcut. Consider, for example, the following:

1. Enter a number.

2. Push the ADD button.

3. Are there any more numbers?

4. If yes, go back to step 1.

How many numbers would this little block of logic add together? How many numbers do we have? Our straw person, following these four instructions, would accumulate values until there were no more values to accumulate. In programming terminology, we'd call this a **loop**.

We might try this logic just to see if, in fact, it works. Take a handful of numbers: 3 + 5 + 2 for example. We know that the correct sum is 10. Let's see if our logic produces that sum. Pick up your pocket calculator and do exactly what the instructions say. Don't clear it; where did you read an instruction that says "Clear the calculator"? Now add 3 + 5 + 2 and get 1347 or some other equally ridiculous answer. Why didn't your logic work? Obviously because you forgot to clear your calculator. By actually trying your solution, you are going through a process known as **desk checking**. It is an invaluable step. No matter how well you think you know what you are doing, there are always going to be little details that you will overlook. The only sure way to catch these oversights is by actually trying your logic. In fact, try it twice; the calculator just might have been cleared by the previous user and you might have missed this problem completely.

Adding the initialization step leads to the following five steps:

1. Clear calculator.

2. Enter a number.

3. Push the ADD button.

4. Are there any more numbers?

5. If yes, go back to step 2.

Now, desk checking should clearly indicate that if we follow the instructions "to the letter" we will successfully add any number of values.

What next? What do we do after there are no more numbers? It's time to divide the accumulated sum of values by the number of values to get the average. We might add step 6, as follows:

6. Divide sum by number of values to get average.

There is only one problem. We know the sum, but how many values were there? Before computing the average, we must count the values. Basically, we have two choices. We can go through our list of values all over again, this time counting instead of accumulating, or we can count values as we go along. The first choice might be reasonable if we have only a few values to average. If we are dealing with hundreds of data points, however, it makes sense to count as we go along. You might imagine yourself making a mark on a paper after adding each number to the accumulator, as in (ⵏ ⵏ llll), or you might use a mechanical counter. Our developing solution now becomes:

1. Clear calculator.

2. Set counter to zero.

3. Enter a number.

4. Push the ADD button.

5. Add 1 to counter.

6. Are there any more numbers?

7. If yes, go back to step 3.

8. Divide accumulator by counter to get average.

9. Copy average onto a sheet of paper.

That last step was added to make certain that a copy of the answer is saved.

We now have a pretty complete average program. The logic should work; desk check it with three or four values to be sure. Try it out on a classmate. Without describing the objective of the program, simply read the instructions, one at a time, and have your friend do exactly what you say. If the answer turns out to be correct, you will *know* that your program works.

Up to this point our objective was simply to define a problem solution in sufficient detail so that we can actually say that we know how to solve the problem. Now that we know what to do, we can begin to discuss how we might adapt this solution to the computer. Before doing this, we must discuss a few very basic computer concepts.

THE COMPUTER

What exactly is a **computer**? Perhaps the best way to answer that question, without getting into unnecessary details, is to compare a computer to its first cousin, the calculator. Imagine actually implementing the problem solution described above on a calculator. Each time the instructions said "Enter a number," you would key in the value and press the "ENTER" button. Each time the instruction said "Push the ADD button," you would press the "ADD" or "+" button. Each step requires you, the human being, to decide what button is to be pressed, and then to press it. The precise steps may be a bit different with a different calculator, but the basic idea of the need for human participation at each and every step is still valid.

Imagine that you have a special machine that automatically pushes the proper buttons in the proper sequence. Given such a machine, calculations could be performed without human intervention. We'd have an automatic calculator. Of course, all the steps would have to be carefully thought out and "programmed" ahead of time, but if a particular set of computations had to be performed over and over again, many many times, the task of preparing the program would be worth the cost. Such an automatic calculator would be, essentially, a computer.

The basic difference between a computer and a calculator is that a computer is designed to function automatically, under control of a program, while a calculator is designed to require step by step human intervention. Basically, a computer is composed of two primary components (Fig. 1.1), a processor and memory. Programs are stored in the computer's memory. The processor performs two basic functions. First, it fetches a single instruction from memory and decodes the instruction, figuring out which specific operation is to be performed; this function is carried out by the control unit portion of the processing unit. Once the control unit has figured out what must be done, it turns control over to an arithmetic and logical unit (Fig. 1.1 again), which does what the instruction says to do. The same thing happens on a calculator, only you provide the control. At some point, you must decide which button to push, thus performing the function of the control unit. When you make up your mind, you push the button, and the calculator performs the function of the arithmetic and logical unit.

A computer is capable of executing a very limited set of instructions. Most computers can:

1. add two numbers,

2. subtract one number from another,

3. multiply two numbers,

4. divide one number into another.

6

Fig. 1.1: *The primary components of a computer.*

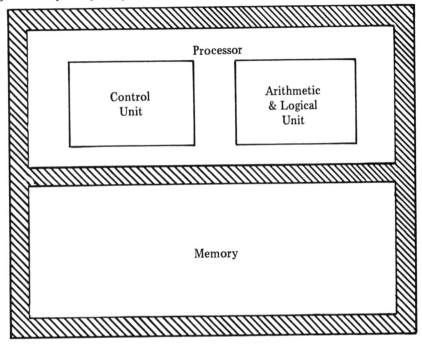

5. copy data from one memory location to another,

6. perform simple yes/no logic,

7. request the input of some data,

8. request the output of some data.

That's about it. A computer program is nothing more than a series of these very simple operations. Of course, they had better be the right operations, and they had better be in the right sequence, but basically that's all a program is.

A few of the computer's instructions need a bit more explanation. Addition, subtraction, multiplication, and division are obvious, so no additional detail is needed, but what is the copy function? Computers are not restricted to numeric data; they can process letters of the alphabet, punctuation marks, and numerous other forms of data as well. Imagine rearranging your laboratory notes into attractive tables and well-spaced prose. The computer, acting under control of the copy or "move" instruction, can do much the same thing, preparing attractive, well-spaced computer print-outs.

What about the computer's yes/no logic capability? Look back at our human-level solution to the average problem. In step 6, we asked, "Are there any more numbers?" Step 7 said, "If yes, go back to step 2". That's yes/no logic. The computer can do much the same thing, checking to see if one number is bigger than another or if one letter comes before another in the alphabet. As we get into the FORTRAN language, we'll begin to discover just how powerful this skill really is.

Input and output may well be new concepts to many of you. Let's once again return to our calculator analogy and see if we can develop a parallel. An early step in our average program called for us to enter a number. What does this step entail? Basically, as you can probably imagine, you key in a number one digit at a time and, when you're finished, you hit a button. That's input. You are providing the calculator with an element of data that it does not already have. After computing the average, you probably copy the answer onto a sheet of paper. That's output; you are transferring information from the calculator to some other medium. Input implies data going into the device; output implies answers or other results coming out from it.

Terminals (Fig. 1.2) are frequently used for getting data into and out from a computer. Imagine that you are a terminal operator. As the computer goes through its program (don't forget, it is working automatically, under control of a pre-supplied program) it eventually encounters an instruction that says, "Read input data." At this point, you, the terminal operator, would be asked to type a number or some other data (depending on the problem being solved) on your terminal and hit the RETURN key, thus sending the data into the computer. Later, when the computer encountered an instruction that told it to write output, the results would be printed on your terminal.

The terminal shown in Fig. 1.2 is a printing terminal; it resembles an electric typewriter. Another very popular type of terminal, resembling a television set with an attached keyboard, is shown in Fig. 1.3. Rather than printing input and output data, such CRT (for cathode ray tube) terminals display the characters on a screen.

One of the best known of all the computer input devices is the card reader. A card reader (Fig. 1.4), as the name implies, reads punched cards (Fig. 1.5). As we'll see later, data is stored in a card by punching a pattern of holes that stand for letters, digits, and punctuation marks. With a card reader as the input device, when the computer encounters an input instruction, it tells the card reader to transfer one cardfull of data into the computer and store it in memory.

The printer (Fig. 1.6) is perhaps the best known computer output device. A printer is used to prepare printed reports under control of the computer. When the computer encounters an output instruction, it normally sends one full line of output information to the printer.

Numerous other input and output devices could be cited, but the beginning programmer will typically submit programs via a terminal or punched cards.

Storing the Program

Several times in the above discussion, we've mentioned that the computer acts under the control of a program. Where is this program found? How does the program get into the computer?

Let's deal with the first question first. The program is normally found in the computer's memory (Fig. 1.7). The control unit portion of the main processor, as you

Fig. 1.2: *A Terminal.*

Courtesy of Anderson Jacobson, Inc.

Fig. 1.3: *A CRT Terminal.*

Courtesy of Control Data Corporation.

Fig. 1.4: *A Card Reader.*

Fig. 1.5: *A Punched Card.*

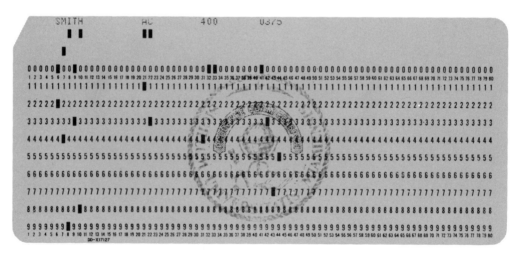

10

Fig. **1.6**: *A Printer.*

Courtesy of Dataproducts Corporation
Woodland Hills, California.

Fig. **1.7**: *A computer with a program and data in main memory.*

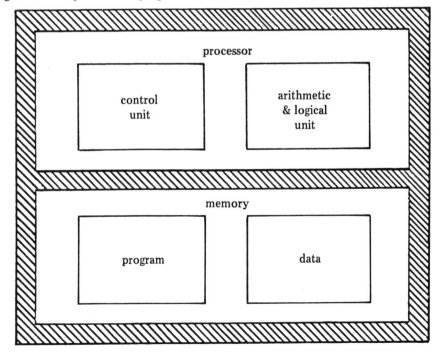

may recall, fetches an instruction from main memory and decodes it, passing control on to the arithmetic and logical unit, which executes the instruction. Then, it's back to the control unit, where another cycle begins. For this cycle to work, the program *must* be in main memory.

How does it get there? This question is not quite so easy. Imagine, to over simplify things a bit, that you have very carefully typed your program, and recorded a copy on a tape cassette. You load this cassette into the computer's tape reader, push a button on the computer's control console, and the program is copied into main memory.

Some smaller computers work exactly this way. On larger computers, programs are stored on high-speed magnetic disk devices, and access is controlled by professional operators and special control programs, but the basic idea is the same.

Storing the Data

What about the data? Where is it stored? Generally, what happens is that, on input, the data is also stored in main memory (Fig. 1.7). While in main memory, the data is processed; in other words, the data is moved around, and arithmetic is performed on it. When output is called for, the results are transferred from main memory to an output device.

The Computer: a Summary

In brief, that's what a computer is: a machine capable of performing a number of logical functions—arithmetic, copying, simple yes/no logic, input, and output. More importantly, it is possible for a human being to write a program consisting of a series of these logical functions and to introduce this program into the computer's main memory; once this has been done, the machine is capable of following the instructions of the program without further human intervention. In effect, given a program to provide control, a computer becomes an automatic machine. For any well defined, highly repetitive task, it's a very valuable machine, indeed.

PLANNING A COMPUTER SOLUTION

We now know how to compute an average by hand. We also know a little bit about the computer. The next step is to develop a plan for implementing our solution on the computer.

Programmers use a number of different tools to aid in this detailed planning step; flowcharting is one of the more commonly used tools.

Flowcharting

A **flowchart** is a graphic representation of a program. Program logic (in other words, the arithmetic, the copy steps, the yes/no logic, and the input and output steps) is defined by using a few standard symbols (Fig. 1.8). These symbols are connected by lines to indicate the flow of logic through the program. Let's say, for example, that we want to read a card containing two numbers, to add the numbers, and to print the

Fig. 1.8: *Flowcharting Symbols.*

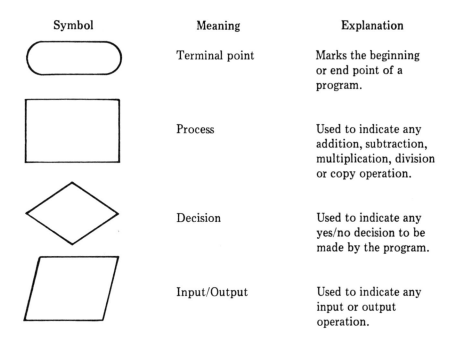

Symbol	Meaning	Explanation
	Terminal point	Marks the beginning or end point of a program.
	Process	Used to indicate any addition, subtraction, multiplication, division or copy operation.
	Decision	Used to indicate any yes/no decision to be made by the program.
	Input/Output	Used to indicate any input or output operation.

sum. A flowchart for this logic is illustrated in Fig. 1.9. Note that the flowchart very clearly defines two things. First, the symbols identify the individual logical steps in the program. Second, by following the lines connecting the symbols, the sequence of these steps is clearly defined. In other words, in addition to telling what must be done, a flowchart also defines the order in which these steps must be performed.

A few simple, generally accepted rules govern the flowlines. The normal direction of flow is from top to bottom or from left to right; arrowheads are used if the direction of flow is anything else. Flowlines should not cross. In general, the idea is to keep things as simple and as straightforward as is possible. To improve the readability of our flowcharts, we will follow the practice of always using arrowheads to indicate the direction of flow.

Look back at the manual solution we developed. Most of the instructions in that solution are pretty straightforward. "Enter a number" is obviously an input operation. "Push the ADD button" just as obviously calls for the execution of an addition operation. Almost without exception, the manual instructions have a direct match with the list of computer instructions presented earlier.

There is, however, one exception. Manual instruction 6 asks the question, "Are there any more numbers?" How do you know that there are no more numbers to be processed? Simple, says the human being, there are no more numbers to be processed. It's not that easy for a computer. The computer, don't forget, gets its data through an input device.

The human being operating the terminal would certainly recognize the fact that there are no more data *before* he or she tries to enter that data. The only way the computer can tell that there are no more data, however, is by asking the programmer or operator to enter some, only to be told that there are none. In other words, the computer cannot look ahead. It can react only to what has happened, and not to what is going to happen. This simple fact forces us to change our view of the problem solution.

Let's flowchart how a computer would have to make the "no more data" decision (Fig. 1.10). Our flowchart begins with an input instruction. Following input, we ask a question: Is this the last of the data? There are two possible responses: yes or no. If the answer is "no," we process the data. If the answer is "yes," we perform end of data processing.

The fact that the end-of-data condition has been reached must be clearly and precisely communicated to the computer. How might the end-of-data test be implemented? Imagine, for example, that there are exactly 50 numbers to be averaged. The programmer might write instructions to count the number of data elements read; the end-of-data condition would then occur when this counter reached 50. Imagine instead that the task is to find the average of a number of examination grades ranging from a possible low of zero to a possible high of 100. After all the valid data have been entered, the operator might type an "impossible" value such as a negative number or a number exceeding 100 to indicate "end-of-data". Simple yes/no logic could then allow the program to test for this "impossible" condition.

In developing a solution to the "average" problem discussed in this chapter, we'll assume that we will be working with a set of positive numbers. After the last valid element of data has been read, we'll enter a negative number to indicate end-of-data. In Chapter 2, we'll see how a test for this condition can be implemented in FORTRAN.

Now we're ready to convert the human-level solution to the average problem into flowchart form. The finished flowchart might look like Figure 1.11. Let's go through it step by step; the steps have been numbered to aid in this process. Follow the flowchart carefully as we move through the program, and be sure that you understand exactly what happens in each and every step. The steps are:

1. This is the start of the program.

2. The accumulator is set ot zero.

3. The counter is set to zero.

Fig. **1.9**: *A simple flowchart.*

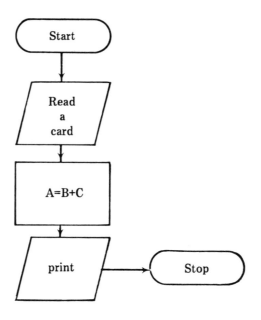

Fig. **1.10**: *Testing for the "end-of-data" condition.*

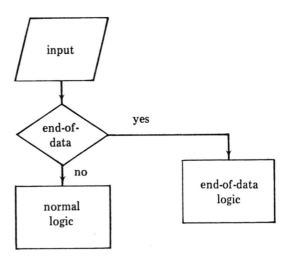

4. Read a value.

5. Test for end-of-data. Why do we want to test for end-of-data before accumulating and counting? Do we want to count the "impossible" negative value? Do we want to accumulate it? No.

6. If this is the end-of-data, skip to instruction 10, where we will compute the average.

7. If it's not, add the number to the accumulator.

8. Add 1 to the counter.

9. Go back and read another value (return to step 4).

10. Divide the accumulator by the counter to get the average. We reached this point, don't forget, only after the end-of-data condition had been encountered.

11. Send a line of output to the terminal.

12. End the program.

Our flowchart formally defines the logic of the soon-to-be-written program. We have used flowcharting as a planning aid, but it serves another important function as well. At some time in the future when we want to look back at our program and perhaps make some modifications, the flowchart serves as a reference document, clearly describing the logical flow of the program in an easy to follow form. Most programs, particularly business programs, will change over time. Thus, documentation is essential, and the flowchart is a very valuable documentation tool.

Defining the Data Fields

The flowchart defines the logical flow of the program, but if a computer is actually to execute this program, the programmer must define more than just the logic. Look back at Fig. 1.7, which shows both the program and the data being stored in main memory. We have a pretty good idea of what the program will contain, but what about the data?

Go through the flowchart (Fig. 1.11) once more, this time concentrating on the data. Block number 2 tells us to set the accumulator to zero; to do that, we must have an accumulator. The next block identifies a counter; we'll need a counter, too. Block number 4 tells us to read a value from the terminal. When that value comes into the computer, there must be space in main memory to hold it. Block number 7 refers to the value and the accumulator; we've already identified both. A similar argument can be advanced for adding a constant (1) to the counter; nothing new here, either. In block number 10, we discover that the average is computed by dividing the accumulator by the counter. Only the average is a new field. Thus, in writing this program, we are going to have to allow for the following data fields:

Fig. 1.11: *A flowchart of the Average Problem.*

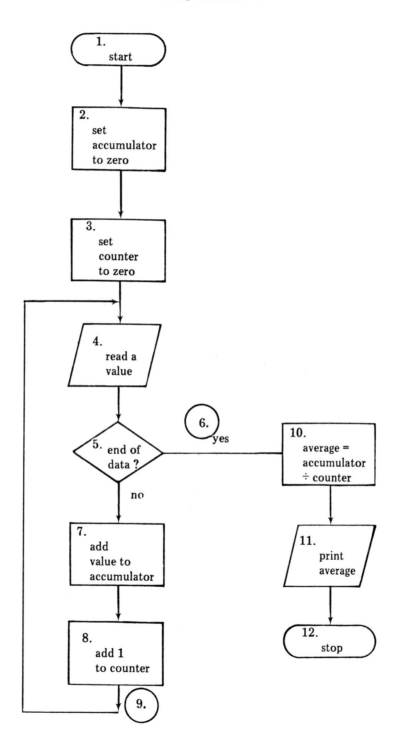

1. an accumulator,

2. a counter,

3. an input value,

4. the computed average.

Why bother defining the data fields before starting to write the code? For one thing, it helps you to avoid confusion. As you begin writing FORTRAN code, you will initially find the syntax of the language troublesome. Defining the data fields first, means that you have one less thing to worry about as you write the program. Later, as your skill increases, you will be writing larger and more complex programs. Once again, it helps to work with pre-defined data fields.

Later, you will learn that more than one type of data can be manipulated on a computer. While we won't get into the details now, you will discover that distinguishing between character and numeric data is crucial, and defining the data fields first is by far the safest way to do it.

CONVERTING OUR PLAN TO A COMPUTER PROGRAM

Finally, we are ready to begin writing the FORTRAN code. At this stage, we have defined the logical flow of the program (through a flowchart) and the data fields that are to be manipulated by the program. Once these factors have been defined, coding (as we'll see in Chapter 2) becomes little more than an exercise in translation.

SUMMARY

This chapter illustrated a reasonable approach for developing a computer-level solution to a problem. We began by carefully defining the problem to be solved. Next, we set up a straw person and planned a manual solution designed to tell this individual how to solve the problem. Throughout this discussion, we emphasized the value of desk checking.

After solving the problem at a human level, we were ready to move along to a computer-level solution. First, however, we found it necessary to describe a few basic computer concepts. A computer is capable of performing arithmetic, copying data from one memory location to another, performing simple yes/no logic, asking for input, and asking for output. The computer is a unique device in that it performs these functions automatically, under the direct control of a program stored in the computer's memory. A program is nothing more than a series of instructions, written by a programmer, designed to guide the computer through some logical function. Various input and output devices can be attached to a computer; we concentrated on terminals, card readers, and printers.

Moving from a manual solution to a computer program, we went through a number of detailed planning steps. First, using flowcharting as a planning aid, we carefully defined the logic of the program. Of particular interest was the way a computer recognizes the fact that the last of the data has been read. Once the logic was defined, we moved along to the data, defining all the data fields to be manipulated by the program. Having laid the ground work, we are now ready to code the program in FORTRAN, the topic of Chapter 2.

EXERCISES

1. An instructor would like to apply a grade curve to an exam so that the class average comes out to exactly 78. This means that if the actual class average is greater than 78, points will be deducted from every student's score and, if the actual average is less than 78, points will be added to every student's score. The easiest way to do this is to find the actual average and then to compute the difference between this figure and the target of 78. How would you modify the problem solution developed in this chapter to implement the extra computation? Add the new computation to the flowchart. The output will now consist of the computed average, and the difference between this average and 78.

2. A baseball player's batting average is computed by dividing the number of times at bat into the number of hits. Since hits cannot possibly exceed times at bat, this statistic will always be a fraction (exception: 1.000); usually it's computed correct to three decimal places. Plan a computer-level solution, including a flowchart, to produce a list of the player number, times at bat, hits, and computed batting average of each of the 25 players on a team.

3. An instructor has indicated that each student's final grade will be computed according to the following formula:

$$
\begin{array}{ll}
\text{exam no. 1} & \ldots\ldots\ldots\ldots 25\% \\
\text{exam no. 2} & \ldots\ldots\ldots\ldots 25\% \\
\text{homework} & \ldots\ldots\ldots\ldots 20\% \\
\text{final exam} & \ldots\ldots\ldots\ldots 30\%
\end{array}
$$

Assume that your actual grades for each of these four grade factors will be typed into a terminal (actual grades are on a scale of 0 - 100). Plan a computer-level solution to read the four grades, compute the percentage value of each of the factors, sum the factor values, and print this final "total grade points" value.

4. A common computer application involves printing address labels for mailings. Assume that you have a series of names and addresses written on a deck of 3 x 5 cards, one name and address per card. Assume that the straw person of this chapter is your secretary, and prepare a set of instructions telling this individual how to prepare properly addressed envelopes from these cards. Once you have completed the human-level instructions, expand your planning to a computer-level solution.

5. Every student knows how his or her school computes a grade point average. Plan a computer-level solution to the problem of computing your own. Your solution should be general; in other words, do *not* assume that the list of courses and associated credit hours and grades are known before the computation begins. If your school uses letter grades, you may convert to a numerical equivalent on input, replacing A's with 4's, B's with 3's, and so on.

6. Imagine that a student is to be paid 1 cent today, 2 cents tomorrow, 4 cents the day after, and so on, with each day's pay exactly doubling that of the day before. How would you go about computing the total amount (cumulative) earned by the student after 30 days? Develop a flowchart.

7. Develop a flowchart for a program to make change. The program should accept the amount paid and the amount of purchase; the total change due is the difference between these two numbers. The logic should, given this amount of change, determine the proper number of dollars, quarters, dimes, nickels, and pennies due the customer.

8. There are four scales to measure temperature: Fahrenheit, Celsius, Kelvin, and Rankine. We want to generate a conversion table. For Fahrenheit temperatures ranging from $0°$ to $222°$ in intervals of $10°$, list the equivalent temperature in the other three scales. You will, of course, need conversion factors; you should be able to find them in any chemistry book or in an encyclopedia. Develop a flowchart.

9. Develop a flowchart for a program to compute and print the sum of the first 200 integers.

10. As we enter the 1980s, the population of the United States is estimated to be 226 million, while Mexico's population is estimated at 66 million. Assume that our population growth rate is 0.9%, while Mexico's is 2.8%. In what year will Mexico pass the United States in population if these trends continue? Develop the algorithms and a flowchart to solve this problem.

2

Writing the Program in FORTRAN

OVERVIEW

In Chapter 1, we developed a solution to a problem. In this chapter we will write the "average" program in the FORTRAN language, and then show you how to execute the program on a computer.

THE FUNCTION OF A PROGRAM

The basic difference between a computer and a calculator is that a calculator requires human intervention at each step in a process, while a computer works automatically, under the control of a program stored in its main memory. The program consists of a series of instructions. Each instruction tells the computer to do one thing: add, subtract, compare, and so on.

A computer's basic function is processing data. Consider, for example, the average program we are about to write. The data consist of a series of numbers. The program will consist of a series of instructions designed to accumulate and count these numbers, to compute their average, and to print the result. Specific instructions, executed in a specific sequence will lead to the desired result. The starting point is the data, the numbers. The objective is the computed average. The program's function is to control the computer as it processes the data into the desired output information.

Of course, the instructions must be written in a form that the computer can understand. Inside the machine, everything—programs and data—is stored in binary form. At one time, programmers actually had to code in pure binary, machine language form, but the modern programmer writes in any of a number of more human-like languages that can be translated to binary by the computer itself. FORTRAN, the FORmula TRANslator, is such a language. Its statements resemble algebraic expressions.

FORTRAN DATA

The key function of a program is to process data. The data is first stored in main memory. The program's instructions manipulate that data; the results are then available for output.

A computer's main memory is divided into a number of independently accessable memory locations. Each element of data occupies one or more such locations. In our average program, for example, we will set aside space to hold the input value, the counter, the accumulator, and the computed average. How do we indicate our need for space to hold these elements of data? How do we differentiate between the space set aside to hold the counter, and the space set aside to hold the accumulator?

In the FORTRAN language, we solve both problems by defining a variable name for each element of data used by the program. The rules for defining variable names are very simple:

1. The first character of the name must be a letter of the alphabet.

2. Only capital letters (A-Z) and digits (0-9) can be used to form a variable name.

3. No more than six characters may be used.

Valid variable names would include A, A1, RADIUS, NUMBER, N5, and so on. In writing the average program, we might define the following variable names:

ACCUM	the accumulator
COUNT	the counter
X	the input value
AVG	the computed average (or mean)

The choice of variable names is up to the programmer. It makes sense, however, to use names that imply something about the use of the element of data. In defining a variable to hold the average for example, AVG is better than WXYZ simply because AVG implies that the variable will hold an average. Note that WXYZ is perfectly legal. The choice of an intelligent variable name is strictly for the convenience of the programmer; it really doesn't matter to the computer.

The FORTRAN programmer must learn to deal with several different types of data. An **integer** is a whole number, with no fractional part; –1, 0, 1, 10, and 132 are examples. A **real number** has a fractional part; 1.5, –15.75, 123.456, and (yes) 10.0 are examples. The computer tends to be most efficient when dealing with integers. Real numbers allow the programmer to store very large, very small, and fractional values.

How can the programmer distinguish between real and integer variables? By convention integer variables begin with one of the letters I, J, K, L, M, or N. Any variable that begins with a different letter, A through H, or O through Z, is real.

EXPRESSIONS

By combining variables, constants, and operators, the FORTRAN programmer can code **expressions**, and thus instruct the computer to perform complex arithmetic operations.

What exactly is a **constant**? A constant is an element of data whose value does not change. Integer constants are numbers that are written without a decimal point: 1, 14, –8, 1342, and 0, for example. Real constants are written with a decimal point; 1.5, 72.3, and –12.5 are examples. Another form of real constant resembles scientific notation; we'll examine such constants, and any limits that might be placed on the size of a constant, in Module A, immediately following this chapter.

Operators are used to specify arithmetic operations. The FORTRAN arithmetic operators are:

+	for addition
−	for subtraction
*	for multiplication
/	for division
**	for exponentiation (raising to a power)

Given the rules for FORTRAN variables, constants, and operators, a FORTRAN expression looks very much like an algebraic expression. For example, the formula for computing the area of a circle is:

$$\text{area} = \pi \, (\text{radius})^2$$

An equivalent FORTRAN expression would be:

3.1416 * RADIUS ** 2

The constant 3.1416 is a real constant simply because it contains a decimal point. The asterisk (*) indicates that multiplication is to be performed. RADIUS is a real variable. How do we know that it is real? It begins with the letter R (perhaps more accurately, it does *not* begin with I, J, K, L, M, or N). The double asterisk (**) indicates that the RADIUS is to be raised to a power; specifically, it is to be squared. The constant 2 is an integer constant. How do you know? It does *not* contain a decimal point.

The Sequence of Operations

In what order are arithmetic operations performed? It does make a difference. Consider, for example, the following simple expression:

5 * 2 + 2.

If the expression is evaluated from left to right, the multiplication is done first (5 * 2 = 10), and then the addition is done (10 + 2 = 12); the answer is 12. If, on the other hand, the expression is evaluated from right to left, the addition will be done first (2 + 2 = 4), followed by the multiplication (5 * 4 = 20), yielding an answer of 20. Obviously both cannot be correct. The order does make a difference.

The rules for determining the order in which the operations in a FORTRAN expression will be performed are the same rules you learned in algebra:

1. raising a value to a power (exponentiation) is first,

2. multiplication and division are second,

3. addition and subtraction are last.

What if there are two additions or a multiplication and a division in a single expression? When such "ties" occur, the operations are performed from left to right. Clearly, 12 is the correct value for the expression described above.

These rules are not always adequate. Consider, for example, a problem in which the sum of two variables, A + B, is to be multiplied by the constant 2. The expression:

A + B * 2

would yield the wrong answer because, given the rules, the multiplication (B * 2) would be done first. We can get around the problem by using parentheses; for example:

(A + B) * 2

Just as in algebra, anything that is enclosed within a set of parentheses must be done first.

Now, consider a more complex expression, such as:

((A + B) * C) ** 2

A set of parentheses surrounds the terms ((A + B) * C), but inside this set of parentheses is another set! What comes first? The rules do not change: do what is within the parentheses. Thus, the first step is to add A and B, which completes the operation specified within the inner parentheses. Now, multiplication can be performed. Finally, when all functions within the parentheses are complete, the result can be raised to the second power.

Most versions of FORTRAN allow the programmer to nest as many as seven sets of parentheses. If, however, an expression becomes so complex that it requires several levels of parentheses, that expression can become very difficult to understand. Thus, it is often better to write a complex function as a series of FORTRAN statements, each one computing part of the answer. A series of simple instructions is almost always better than a single complex instruction.

ASSIGNMENT STATEMENTS

An expression, by itself, is incomplete. Coding:

$$3.1416 * RADIUS ** 2$$

is fine, but what are we to do with the answer? In a FORTRAN assignment statement, such as:

$$AREA = 3.1416 * RADIUS ** 2$$

the value of the expression is assigned to the variable on the left side of the equal sign.

What is an assignment statement? Consider the following two statements:

$$ACCUM = 0.0$$

$$COUNT = 0.0$$

What do they do? The first statement says to copy whatever is on the right side of the equal sign into the memory location specified on the left side of the equal sign; in other words, to copy the constant 0.0 (a real constant) into the memory location named ACCUM. The second statement says much the same thing, copying 0.0 into the memory location to which the name COUNT has been assigned.

The assignment statement:

$$AREA = 3.1416 * RADIUS ** 2$$

has a similar meaning. It tells the computer to square the value found in memory location RADIUS, multiply the result by the constant 3.1416, and then to copy or assign the answer to the memory location called AREA.

Note that we have very carefully avoided using the phrase "is equal to" in the above discussion. The equal sign does not mean what it means in algebra. For example, the statement:

$$COUNT = COUNT + 1.0$$

violates the rules of algebra, but it is perfectly legal (and quite common) in FORTRAN. The statement tells the computer to take whatever value is stored in the memory location named COUNT, add 1 to it, and store the sum at the memory location named COUNT.

The general form of an assignment statement is:

> variable = expression

The equal sign means "is replaced by". The content of the variable coded on the left side of the equal sign is replaced by the value of the expression on the right side.

THE SEQUENCE OF INSTRUCTIONS

It is one thing to write a valid assignment statement. It is quite a different thing to determine what statement should be written "next". A FORTRAN program consists of a series of FORTRAN statements, and both the individual statements and their order must be correct if the program is to produce the desired output.

One of the first rules you must learn as you begin to write programs is that the computer assumes nothing. Consider, for example, the statement:

X = Y + Z

What is the value of X? Unless you know the values of Y and Z, you have no way of answering this question. Neither does the computer. In other words, that statement, all by itself, is meaningless.

Consider instead the following series of instructions:

Y = 10.0

Z = 20.0

X = Y + Z

Now, what is the value of X? The answer, clearly, is 30.0.

The point is very simple. The value of every term on the right side of the equal sign must be known *before* an assignment statement is coded. In the statement:

Y = 10.0

the number 10 is a constant, and the value of a constant is always known. The statement:

X = Y + Z

is valid only if previous statements have assigned values to both Y and Z. Failure to follow this simple rule is a common source of error among beginners.

THE READ STATEMENT

Typically, the data to be processed exist as numbers on a sheet of paper, or holes punched in a series of cards, or values recorded on some other medium. Before this data can be processed, it must be transferred into the computer. In FORTRAN, input operations are controlled by a **READ** statement. The basic form of the READ statement is:

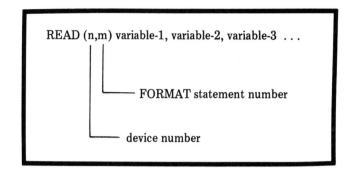

READ (n,m) variable-1, variable-2, variable-3 . . .

            FORMAT statement number

        device number

FORTRAN is a general purpose language used on a variety of computer systems. Input can come from a card reader, a terminal, a tape drive, or any of numerous other devices. The device number allows the programmer to specify the device. The beginner will typically use a card reader or a terminal; devices 2 or 5 are commonly used.

A FORMAT statement is used to describe the position-by-position contents of an input or output record. We'll be covering FORMAT statements in Chapter 3 and in Module B (which follows Chapter 3). For now, we'll be using unformatted input and output (called list-directed I/O), so we'll code an asterisk (*) to indicate the absence of a FORMAT statement number. Following the parentheses that surround the device number and FORMAT statement number, any number of variable names can be coded, separated by commas.

Earlier, in illustrating the significance of the sequence of instructions in a program, we coded a series of three assignment statements:

$$Y = 10.0$$

$$Z = 20.0$$

$$X = Y + Z$$

We could have written:

READ (5,*) Y, Z

X = Y + Z

The READ statement would have caused the computer to go out to device number 5 (the card reader), get two values from a punched card, and assign the values to the space set aside for variables Y and Z respectively. The assignment statement would then add the two values and place the answer in X.

When using unformatted or list-directed I/O, how is the data coded? Basically, a list of data values is set up separated by commas or blank spaces. The input card for the READ statement described above might, for example, contain:

12.0,15.5

Given this card (or terminal line), the value 12.0 would be assigned to Y, and the value 15.5 would be assigned to Z.

OUTPUT: THE WRITE STATEMENT

The whole point of using the computer is to process input data into output information that can be used by some human being. Without output, the process is rather pointless. FORTRAN output is controlled by the **WRITE** statement:

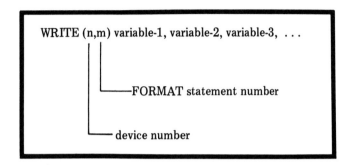

The device number and FORMAT statement number have the same meaning as in a READ statement. Common device numbers for a printer or a terminal are 3 and 6. Once again, any number of variable names, separated by commas, can be coded following the parentheses.

FORTRAN 77 supports a simplier form of list-directed output statement, the PRINT statement. By coding:

PRINT * ,AVG

the computer can be instructed to print the current value stored in the memory location named AVG. We will use the general form of the WRITE statement, however, coding

WRITE (6,*) AVG

Once again, the asterisk is used to indicate the absence of a FORMAT statement number.

CONTROL STATEMENTS

Computers are most valuable when performing repetitive logic. A problem is solved once. The program instructions are then executed over and over again, in a loop.

There is only one problem. The computer normally executes its instructions in straight sequence. A loop structure implies that several instructions will be executed in normal sequence, and then control will return to the top of the loop, so that they can be repeated. The "return to the top" step is a violation of the normal sequence, and there must be a mechanism for achieving this "branch" or jump. That mechanism is the **GO TO** statement:

```
GO TO   statement-number
```

For example, as part of our average program, we might code:

```
10 READ (5,*) X

   ACCUM = ACCUM + X

   COUNT = COUNT + 1.0

   GO TO 10
```

The integer number in front of the READ statement is a *statement number*. It serves to identify the statement. Responding to the READ, the computer will get a value from the card reader. Then, the value will be accumulated and counted. Finally, the GO TO statement will return control to the READ statement (number 10), and the loop will be repeated.

A statement number is needed only when a given statement is referenced from another part of the program. For example, the target of a GO TO statement must always have a number. The statement number must be a positive integer between 1 and 99999. Numbers need not be assigned in any particular sequence. Once a number is used, however, you may not use it again in the same program.

There is only one thing wrong with the logic coded above; there is no way out of that loop. Those four statements will be endlessly executed over and over again. When do we want to terminate the loop? When we run out of data. How can we identify that condition? Since, in this problem, we are assuming that the numbers to be averaged are all positive, the programmer can simply enter a negative number to signify the end of data. Now all we need is a mechanism that allows the program to recognize a negative number.

That mechanism is the IF statement. There are several forms of IF statements in FORTRAN 77. The arithmetic IF and the logical IF will be covered briefly in Module A. Most of the examples in this text will be coded using a different form of the IF statement that is new to FORTRAN 77, the IF. . .THEN. . .ELSE logic block. The general form of an IF. . .THEN. . .ELSE block is:

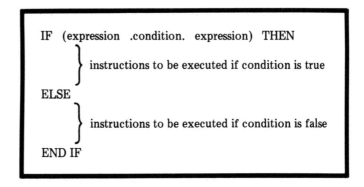

IF (expression .condition. expression) THEN

} instructions to be executed if condition is true

ELSE

} instructions to be executed if condition is false

END IF

Any valid FORTRAN expression can be used, although most programmers tend to compare simple variables and constants for clarity. Valid conditions include:

.EQ.	equal to
.LT.	less than
.GT.	greater than
.LE.	less than or equal to
.GE.	greater than or equal to
.NE.	not equal to

An IF. . .THEN. . .ELSE block is the programmer's basic conditional logic block. A condition is tested. That condition is either true, or it is false. If true, the THEN logic is executed. If false, the ELSE logic is executed. That's all there is to it.

In our average program, the purpose of the IF statement will be to test for the end of data condition (a negative number). What do we want to do when the end of data condition is encountered? Compute the average and end the program. We might code the following logic block:

```
IF (X .LT. 0.0) THEN

        AVG = ACCUM / COUNT

        WRITE (6,*) AVG

        STOP

ELSE

END IF
```

The condition being tested is "X is less than 0.0". If this condition is true, the assignment statement that computes the average will be executed, followed by the WRITE statement and the STOP statement (which clearly marks the end of the program). If the condition is not true, nothing happens (there are no statements between the ELSE and the END IF), and the program simply follows its normal course. Adding this block to the loop coded earlier yields:

```
10  READ (5,*) X

    IF (X .LT. 0.0) THEN

                AVG = ACCUM / COUNT

                WRITE (6,*) AVG

                STOP

        ELSE

        END IF

    ACCUM = ACCUM + X

    COUNT = COUNT + 1.0

    GO TO 10
```

ENDING THE PROGRAM

We have already used the instruction that marks the logical end of a program—STOP. A statement number can be attached to a STOP statement, allowing the programmer to GO TO it. The last statement executed by your program must be a STOP.

The very last statement in your program must be an **END statement**. An END statement and a STOP statement are different. Remember that statements written in a language such as FORTRAN cannot be directly executed by a computer; they must first be translated into binary, machine-level code. An END statement tells the FORTRAN compiler that there are no more instructions to be *translated*. The STOP statement is simply another statement during the translation (or compilation) phase, but after the program begins to execute, a STOP statement tells the computer that there are no more instructions to be *executed*. Can you see why you might have several STOP statements in a program, but you can have only one END? The END terminates translation or compilation, while the STOP terminates program execution.

WRITING THE AVERAGE PROGRAM IN FORTRAN

We have now covered all the FORTRAN statements we will need to write the average program. One more statement is, however, worthy of mention, the **comment**. A comment is a note written by the programmer to provide documentation; in other words, a comment is used to explain what the other statements do. Comments are always optional, but you will probably find at least a minimal level of documentation essential. Our practice in this text will be to begin each program with a block of comments identifying the programmer and the function of the program.

Let's turn our attention to the average program. We will be using the following variable names:

ACCUM	accumulator
COUNT	counter
X	the input value
AVG	the computed average

We also have, from Chapter 1, a flowchart (reproduced as Fig. 2.1). Our objective is to convert this flowchart into FORTRAN code.

We'll start with a set of comments:

```
C                 * PROGRAM TO COMPUTE AN AVERAGE
C                 *    WRITTEN BY:  W. S. DAVIS
C                 *            1/8/81
C                 * * * * * * * * * * * * * * * * *
```

The comments identify the program and the programmer. FORTRAN comments start with the letter C in the first position. Why did we skip so many spaces between the letter C and the comment proper? The comments are not really part of the program. They are for documentation, for support. If we shift the comments over to the right, and leave the regular FORTRAN statements aligned on the left, we'll have an obvious visual separation between the primary instructions and the support instructions; in other words, the comments will be able to do their job without getting in the way.

The rules for writing FORTRAN statements are really quite simple. The first five positions of the card or the terminal line are used for coding statement numbers. Column (or position) 6 is usually blank. Positions 7 through 72 are used to hold the FORTRAN statement itself. These coding rules are summarized in Fig. 2.2.

Let's go through the flowchart step by step, writing a FORTRAN statement to implement the logic of each step. First, we must set the accumulator and the counter to zero. We can do this by coding:

Fig. 2.1: *A flowchart of the Average Problem.*

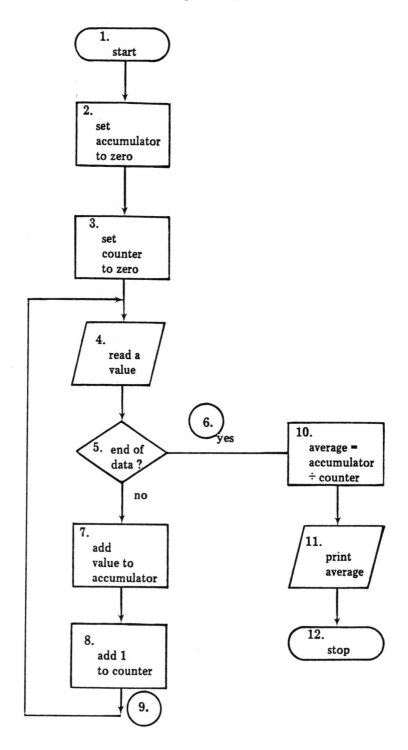

1 → 5	6	7 ——————————————→ 72
stmt. nmbr.	b l a n k	FORTRAN statement

```
ACCUM = 0.0

COUNT = 0.0
```

Following the initialization of these two work fields, we enter the loop that reads, counts, and accumulates values. When the last record is encountered, the average is computed and printed, and the program ends. We coded this loop earlier:

```
10 READ (5,*) X

   IF (X .LT. 0.0) THEN

              AVG = ACCUM / COUNT

              WRITE (6,*) AVG

              STOP

      ELSE

      END IF

   ACCUM = ACCUM + X

   COUNT = COUNT + 1.0

   GO TO 10
```

Combining the comments, the initialization instructions, the loop, and a necessary END statement yields the program shown in Fig. 2.3.

RUNNING THE PROGRAM

Now that the program logic is defined, how do we submit it to the computer? In most cases, the beginning student will use either punched cards or a terminal. Some schools use a key-to-disk system, with students storing programs on diskette; operationally, such systems are similar to punched card systems.

Punched Card Program Submission

To illustrate how a program might be submitted using punched cards, we'll briefly go through an example using a very popular academic compiler, WATFIV-S (the University of *WAT*erloo's *F*ORTRAN *IV*, *S*tructured). Under WATFIV-S, FORTRAN statements are keypunched one to a card, with statement numbers in columns 1-5, column 6 blank (usually), and the FORTRAN instruction in columns 7-72. Remaining card columns are used to hold optional program identification information.

Fig. 2.4 shows a complete deck ready for submission to the WATFIV compiler. It begins with a control card, $JOB. In most cases, a course identification number and a student identification number are punched on this first card. The $JOB card

Fig. 2.3: *The average program in FORTRAN.*

```
C                                    *  PROGRAM TO COMPUTE AN AVERAGE
C                                    *     WRITTEN BY: W.S. DAVIS
C                                    *              1/8/81
C                                    * * * * * * * * * * * * * * * *
      ACCUM = 0.0
      COUNT = 0.0
   10 READ (5.*) X
      IF (X .LT. 0.0) THEN DO
                      AVG = ACCUM/COUNT
                      WRITE (6.*) AVG
                      STOP
         ELSE DO
         END IF
      ACCUM = ACCUM + X
      COUNT = COUNT + 1.0
      GO TO 10
      END
```

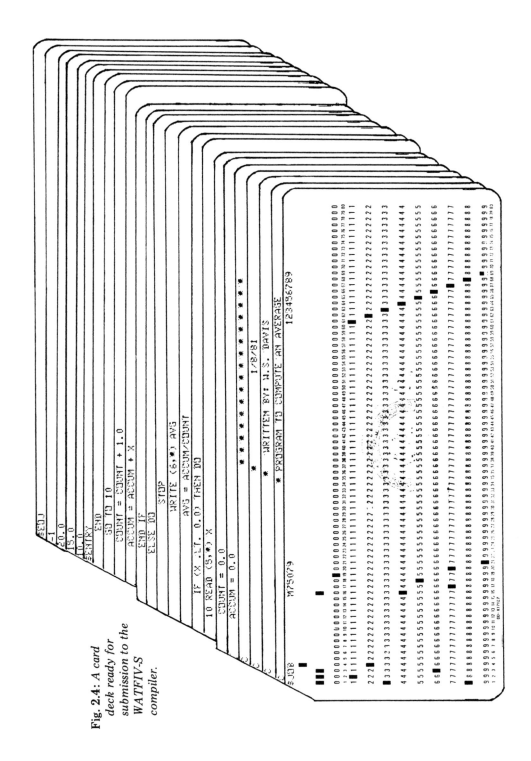

Fig. 2.4: *A card deck ready for submission to the WATFIV-S compiler.*

37

marks the beginning of the program, and tells the computer system that the WATFIV-S compiler is to be loaded and executed. The identification numbers allow the computer to verify that you are an authorized user of the computer. (Computer time is, after all, quite expensive.) The $JOB must begin in column 1 of the card; normally, the course identification number starts in column 16, and the student ID begins in column 61.

Following the first control card are the FORTRAN statements, punched one statement to a card. Note that blank spaces have been used to group statements and to separate the variables, operators, and constants, thus making the statements easier to read. In most versions of FORTRAN, blanks are ignored. Thus, you, the programmer, can use blank spaces at your own convenience, without worrying how FORTRAN might react.

In the IF. . .THEN. . .ELSE block of WATFIV-S the word *DO* follows THEN and ELSE. Otherwise, the program looks much as before. Such minor differences between versions of FORTRAN are quite common.

Following the last statement in the program (an END statement), another control card, a $ENTRY card, is coded. The $ENTRY card serves to separate the FORTRAN program from its data. Executing a program is a two-step process. First, the source statements must be compiled or translated to machine-level code; the $JOB card says, "start compilation". After a machine-level version of the program has been generated, the data can be processed. The $ENTRY card essentially says, "stop compiling and start processing".

The data cards follow the $ENTRY card. Note that each data card contains a single value (Fig. 2.4).

The last card in the program deck must be a $EOJ card. It marks the end of the job, and indicates that all data have been processed.

Unless you are very unusual, you will make an occasional coding or keypunching error. Fig. 2.5 shows the output from a program with such an error. Note that the program statements are listed first. After the $ENTRY an error message is printed: "VALUE OF CONT IS UNDEFINED". Directly under the error message is another comment that identifies the statement that was executing at the time the error was encountered. Line number 11 (the line numbers can be seen at the left of Fig. 2.5) contains the instruction:

COUNT = CONT + 1.0

Clearly, the statement:

COUNT = COUNT + 1.0

is what the programmer intended to code. The solution is to keypunch the instruction correctly, replace the bad instruction, and resubmit the program.

Fig. 2.5: *A program listing with an error message.*

```
$JOB                                        * PROGRAM TO COMPUTE AN AVERAGE
      C                                     *    WRITTEN BY: W.S. DAVIS
      C                                     *           1/8/81
      C                                     * * * * * * * * * * * * * * *
      C
  1           ACCUM = 0.0
  2           COUNT = 0.0
  3        10 READ (5,*) X
  4           IF (X .LT. 0.0) THEN DO
  5                        AVG = ACCUM/COUNT
  6                        WRITE (6,*) AVG
  7                        STOP
  8              ELSE DO
  9              END IF
 10           ACCUM = ACCUM + X
 11           COUNT = CONT + 1.0
 12           GO TO 10
 13           END
      $ENTRY
***ERROR***  VALUE OF CONT    IS UNDEFINED

      PROGRAM WAS EXECUTING LINE     11 IN ROUTINE M/PROG

STATEMENTS EXECUTED=         6
```

Terminal Program Submission

Increasingly, punched card program submission is giving way to terminal-based systems. The mechanics of terminal program submission vary significantly from installation to installation; thus we will leave the technical details to your instructor.

The fact that a terminal is to be used does not change the basic program development process, however. Careful planning must still preceed coding. Many terminal systems are quite "friendly", and seem easy to use. The temptation is to "just sit down and start coding". Don't. Think first.

THE PROGRAM DEVELOPMENT PROCESS

Writing a program consists of at least two clearly identifiable steps. The first is *logical*: What instruction should I write next? This logical function calls for careful planning, and careful thought. Chapter 1 was devoted to this logical function. The second step is largely *mechanical*: How should I write this specific instruction? Chapter 2 was concerned with the mechanics of writing the FORTRAN instructions needed to implement the already planned average program.

Anyone can learn the mechanics of coding; all it takes is practice. The rules and syntax of FORTRAN may seem confusing right now, but if you stick with it, writing the code will become easy. It is just a matter of time and effort.

The real problem is logic. Planning the proper sequence of steps in a program requires careful thought, careful planning, and a moderate degree of aptitude. It is this ability to think, to logically define the solution to a problem as a series of program instructions, that earns a person the title "programmer".

All too often, the beginner tends to lose sight of this essential fact. For obvious reasons, programming texts start with examples involving relatively simple logic—the computation of an average, for example. The logic seems obvious; the task of coding that logic seems relatively difficult, simply because the beginner has never written code before. The result is predictable. The student becomes so concerned with the mechanics that he or she, figuratively, "cannot see the forest for the trees". The *real* problem is defining the correct logic. The *perceived* problem becomes one of writing instructions in FORTRAN (or some other language).

Is this unusual? Not at all. Have you ever known a student whose excessive concern for spelling and punctuation, the mechanics of writing, interfered with the ability to write a decent paper? Have you ever known a student who failed to grasp the underlying concept being presented in an analytical course because of excessive concern with the mechanics of manipulating algebraic symbols? Perhaps you have missed a key idea in a history course because of an excessive concern with names, dates, and places.

How can you avoid this problem as you begin to learn how to program? The answer is really quite simple: *Do your planning first.* Force yourself to:

1. define all key variables or data fields, and

2. define the logical flow of the program using either psuedocode, flowcharts, or both,

before writing a single line of code. If you take the time to do this, the task of coding will be reduced simply to translating already defined operations, one at a time, into the FORTRAN language. The key question: "What instruction should I code next?", will have been answered. In effect, you will have already mapped the forest; then, you can worry about the trees.

Try it. It works.

SUMMARY

Using the FORTRAN language, the average program planned in Chapter 1 was coded. First, it was necessary to present several basic concepts. FORTRAN variables and constants (integer and real), operators, expressions, and assignment statements were explained. READ and WRITE statements are needed to control I/O. GO TO and IF statements allow the programmer to control the order in which instructions are executed. FORTRAN 77 supports an IF. . .THEN. . .ELSE logic structure. A STOP statement marks the logical end of the program; the (physically) last statement in the program must be an END.

To illustrate the task of submitting the program, we used a popular academic compiler: WATFIV-S. Rules for keypunching and sequencing program statements, data, and control cards were covered, and a sample card deck presented. We then considered a program listing with an error message. Terminal program submission is a common alternative; the technical details were left to your instructor.

The chapter ended with a brief discussion of the program development process. This section stressed the value of planning a solution *before* beginning to write code.

Note

Additional FORTRAN syntax details can be found in Module A, immediately following this chapter. You may want to read this material before completing the exercises below.

EXERCISES

1. The formula for finding the area of a circle is:

$$AREA = \pi r^2$$

where $\pi = 3.1416$, and "r" is the radius. Write a program to compute and print the area of a circle of radius 5.25.

2. Modify program 1 so that it computes the area of a circle of any radius. Use a READ statement to provide the value of the radius. Repeat the program for several values, using an IF statement to test for the end of data condition; devise a reasonable test for end of data.

3. The volume of a cylinder can be computed by the formula:

$$v = \pi r^2 h,$$

where $\quad \pi = 3.1416,$

$r = $ radius,

$h = $ height.

Write a program to input the value of radius and height and compute the volume. Print the answer.

4. A baseball player's batting average can be computed by dividing hits by times at bat. Write a program to input, for each player, hits and times at bat, compute the batting average, and then print the player's times at bat, hits, and computed batting average. Note that there might be as few as nine and as many as twenty-five players on the team. Devise a reasonable end of data check.

5. The Pythagorean Theorem says that, given the length of any two sides (a and b) of a right triangle, the formula:

$$c = \sqrt{a^2 + b^2}$$

can be used to find the length of the third side. Write a program to compute and print the length of the third side given the input of the lengths of the other two sides. Note: the square root of X is X ** 0.5.

6. The outer radius of a flat washer is eight inches. The inner radius (the radius of the hole) is six inches. Compute and print the area of the washer.

7. If light travels 186,000 miles per second, how far does it travel in 3.5 years?

8. The area of a triangle can be found by using the formula:

$$area = \sqrt{S\ (S\text{-}a)\ (S\text{-}b)\ (S\text{-}c)}$$

where a, b, and c are the lengths of the three sides, and:

$$S = \frac{a + b + c}{2}$$

Write a program to compute and print the area of a triangle using this formula.

9. In 1626 the Indians sold Manhattan Island to the Dutch for roughly $24. If they had invested this money at 8% interest, what would it be worth today? The formula for computing interest earned is:

$$W = P\ (1 + i)^n$$

where   W = future value (in this case, the value today),

               P = the original investment (in this case, $24),

               i = the interest rate,

               n = the number of years.

10. Write the program planned in exercise 1, Chapter 1.

11. Write Chapter 1, exercise 3.

12. Write Chapter 1, exercise 5.

13. A baseball pitcher's earned run average is computed by using the following formula:

$$ERA = (earned\ runs) / (equivalent\ nine\ inning\ games),$$

where the term (equivalent nine inning games) is computed by dividing the actual innings pitched by nine. Write a program to compute and print the earned run averages for a number of players.

14. A quadratic equation of the form

$$Ax^2 + Bx + C = 0$$

has a pair of solutions which can be computed by solving:

$$x = \frac{-B \pm \sqrt{B^2 - 4AC}}{2A}$$

Write a program to input values for A, B, and C, and compute the two roots. Remember that you cannot take the square root of a negative number. Consider using several simple expressions instead of one complex expression.

Module

FORTRAN Syntax

OVERVIEW

Chapter 1 was concerned with planning a solution to a problem; in Chapter 2, we implemented that solution in the FORTRAN language. The emphasis of these two chapters was on the entire program development process. Coding, the task of actually writing the instructions, is but one step in this process. You can learn to write code. Anyone can learn to write code; all it takes is practice. The real trick to programming is knowing what instruction to write next. If a problem solution has been carefully planned before coding begins, the programmer will know what instruction to code next, and the task of writing the instructions will become a largely mechanical process.

The fact that coding is (or should be) largely mechanical does not, however, mean that it is a trivial problem. The purpose of a program is to tell a computer (a machine) how to perform some function. The instructions that make up the program must be precise, or the computer will be unable to understand them. Coding requires extreme attention to detail. The programmer must follow the syntax rules of the language.

If you are a typical beginner, you will find the rules and syntax of the FORTRAN language a bit confusing at first. This feeling passes, usually with the successful completion of your first program or two. All it takes is practice. That is the purpose of this module: to provide you with some practice in FORTRAN syntax. A number of drill exercises are included; the answers to these drill exercises can be found in the Appendix in the back of the book.

ARITHMETIC EXPRESSIONS

Constants

A constant is a value that does not change throughout the execution of a program. In FORTRAN, there are two kinds of numeric constants: integers and real numbers. An integer is a simple counting number, without a decimal point: 0, 1, -5, 14, and 132 are examples. A real number has a decimal point.

Let's consider integer constants first. The rules for coding such numbers are really quite simple: just write the number with *no* decimal point. If the number is negative, a minus sign (-) *must be* placed in front of the first digit; if the number is positive, the plus sign (+) is optional, and is usually not coded. You *may not* bury commas within the number; for example, 186,000 is illegal in FORTRAN. Code the number without the comma; 186000 is correct. Nonsignificant leading zeros can (optionally) be included, as in 000123, although 123 would be a more common form of the same constant. Most versions of FORTRAN ignore blank spaces. Occasionally, the programmer will wish to take advantage of this fact to clarify the value of a lengthy integer. For example, a social security number such as 123456789 might be coded as 123 45 6789. Your version of FORTRAN *may* treat blanks as zeros, however, so be careful.

There are limits on the size of an integer constant. For example, on a large IBM computer the biggest integer that can be stored is roughly two billion, while the smallest is roughly minus two billion. These limits are a function of the computer system used; check your system reference manual to find the limits for your computer.

Real numbers have a decimal point; 3.1416, 10.0, and -14.5 are examples. If a number is negative, the minus sign must be coded; the plus sign is always optional. Once again, commas may *not* be buried in the constant; only digits and a single decimal point may be coded. On many systems, blanks may be embedded in the constants; on others, blanks are converted to zeros; be careful.

Very large and very small numbers can be represented in scientific notation. For example, the speed of light is roughly 186,000 miles per second. Using scientific notation, this value can be written as 0.186×10^6. The power of ten (in this case, the 6) indicates how many places the decimal point must be moved to the right. Very small numbers can be represented by using a negative power of ten. For example, an angstrom unit is defined as one-hundred millionth of a centemeter, or 0.00000001 centemeter. In scientific notation this value becomes 0.1×10^{-7}. Both the speed of light and the angstrom unit are shown in what is called *normalized* form, with the first significant digit immediately following the decimal point. As an alternative, we could have written 1.86×10^5 and 1.0×10^{-8}; show why these two forms are equivalent to the values shown above.

FORTRAN numeric constants can be coded using a form of scientific notation. The "x10" is present in any number written in scientific form. To code FORTRAN constants, the programmer replaces the "x10" with the letter E. The speed of light can be written as 1.86E5, while the length of an angstrom unit becomes 1.0E-8. Preceeding the letter E is the numeric portion of the constant; following the E is the power of ten. Such numbers are called *real* numbers or *floating-point* numbers.

The limits on a real number vary from system to system. On a large IBM machine, a maximum of seven digits of precision can be obtained, while numbers as big as 10^{74} or as small as 10^{-74} (roughly) can be coded. To put the pieces together, 0.9999999E74 and 0.9999999E–74 are limits. Check the reference manual or ask your instructor for the limits on your system.

There are several other types of constants in FORTRAN, including double precision numbers, complex numbers, logical constants, and character constants. We'll leave them for later, however.

EXERCISES

1. Listed below are several numeric constants. Are they correct or incorrect? If a given constant is correct, is it integer or real? If incorrect, why is it incorrect?

    a. 12   g. +398

    b. 12.0   h. –927

    c. 25.25 1   i. 0.5E50

    d. 123,456   j. 1234567890

    e. 123456.789   k. –1.75751E–63

    f. –123456.   l. 1234567.0E67

2. You should be able to find the values for many of the following in a good dictionary. Write each as a FORTRAN constant.

    a. PI (or π).

    b. A conversion factor for centemeters to inches.

    c. A conversion factor for meters to inches.

    d. A conversion factor for kilometers to miles.

    e. A "straight A" average.

    f. The number of credit hours needed to graduate from your school.

    g. The population of the United States.

    h. The size of an atom.

    i. The distance to the nearest star.

47

j. The length of a light year in miles.

k. The frequency of your favorite radio station.

l. Your hourly pay rate.

m. The sticker-price of a new automobile.

n. The speed (in revolutions per minute) of a long-playing record album.

Variables

The value of a variable can change during execution of a program. Essentially, a variable name represents a storage location. A programmer can cause a value to be stored at the location, or retrieve a previously stored value by referencing the variable name. The FORTRAN rules for assigning variable names are quite simple:

1. The first character must be a letter of the alphabet.

2. Any combination of letters and digits (0-9) may be used.

3. A maximum of six characters may be used.

The programmer may select any variable name he or she chooses as long as the syntax rules are followed. It makes sense, however, to select variable names that mean something. For example, PAY would be better for a pay rate than would L. When computing an average, a variable named AVG would make more sense than one named X. This is for the convenience of the programmer; meaningful variable names make it easier to follow the logic of the program. The computer really doesn't care.

What about variable type? By convention, any variable beginning with I, J, K, L, M, or N is integer; if the variable name begins with any other letter, it is real. The programmer can, however, override this convention. Assume, for example, that the value of net pay is to be computed in a payroll program. Clearly, a monetary amount such as net pay will include a decimal point, and thus will be real. A reasonable name for this field would be NET, but NET is, by convention, integer. By coding:

REAL NET

the programmer states that, in effect, "I don't care what the convention is, NET is a real variable." A similar statement can be used to define a variable as integer, no matter what the first letter might be. This is the INTEGER statement, coded as:

INTEGER var-1, var-2, var-3, . . .

You may code as many variables as you wish after either a REAL or an INTEGER statement.

You must declare the type of a variable *before* you use it. For example, consider the following instructions:

        FIELD = 0.0

        INTEGER FIELD

Note: this sequence is incorrect.

In the first statement, FORTRAN will assume that FIELD is real. Space is set up, and a real value is stored. By the time the INTEGER statement is encountered, it is too late, the action has already been taken. *Always* code your INTEGER and REAL statements *first*, before any executable statements. In fact, many FORTRAN programmers list *all* their variables in INTEGER and REAL statements at the beginning of the program; such variable lists are an important aid to documentation. Incidently, you may code several REAL and several INTEGER statements in a single program if necessary.

EXERCISES

1. Given the following two statements:

        INTEGER X, REAL, A14

        REAL INTG, A27, K

    Which of the following variables are real, which are integer, and which are incorrect? If a variable is incorrect, why is it incorrect?

a.	REAL	g.	INTG
b.	INTEGER	h.	MEAN
c.	PAY	i.	NUMBER
d.	ABC123	j.	IJKL123
e.	K	k.	A14
f.	WRONG	l.	KORECT

2. Earlier in Module A, exercise 2 asked you to find a series of constants (see page 47). Code a meaningful variable name for each of these values.

Operators

Arithmetic operations in FORTRAN are defined by using the following operators:

+   addition

–   subtraction

*   multiplication

/   division

**   exponentiation, involution, or raising to a power

Expressions

An expression is a series of one or more variables and/or constants linked by operators. As we'll learn later, an expression can also include subscripted variables and built-in (intrinsic) functions. The programmer specifies the arithmetic steps the computer is to follow by writing expressions.

To add variables A and B, the programmer would code:

A + B

To multiply X by 4, the following expression:

X * 4

would be coded. The formula for computing the area of a circle is π times the radius squared. A FORTRAN expression for this formula would be:

3.1416 * RADIUS ** 2

Certain arithmetic operations should not be coded, as they can lead to program failure on many systems. Do not:

1. Divide by zero.

2. Raise zero to the zero power.

3. Raise zero to a negative power.

4. Raise a negative number to a non-integer power.

5. Compute a value that exceeds the upper limit of your computer system.

6. Compute a value that is smaller than the lower limit of your computer system.

Such errors are generally not intentional. If your program quits in the middle and the word *overflow* or *underflow* appears on your terminal, or your listing, you may well have violated one of these rules.

Before we move on to more complex expressions, we must first discuss the sequence of operations. Consider, for example, the expression:

6 + 4 / 2

Is the value of the expression 5, or is it 8? The answer depends on the order in which the operations are performed. The correct answer, in this case, is 8, because FORTRAN uses the following sequence rules:

1. Exponentiation (involution) comes first.

2. Multiplication and division come second.

3. Addition and subtraction are done last.

In the event of ties (multiplication *and* division in the same expression, for example) the expression is evaluated from left to right.

What if you wanted the addition to be performed first? As is the case in standard algebra, parentheses can be used to indicate a change in the normal order of computation. The value of the expression:

(6 + 4) / 2

would be 5. Any steps enclosed within the parentheses are done before steps outside the parentheses. Note that the normal sequence rules—exponentiation, multiplication/division, addition/subtraction—are followed within a set of parentheses.

Consider, for example, the following expression:

1.0 + 2.0 * 3.0 / 2.0 ** 2

Exponentiation is done first; the expression is thus reduced to:

1.0 + 2.0 * 3.0 / 4.0

Next comes multiplication. Why is multiplication done before division? Simply because, in the event of ties, computation goes from left to right. We have now reduced the problem to:

1.0 + 6.0 / 4.0

Division comes next; it should be clear that the value of this expression is 2.5.

What if parentheses are used to change the order of computation? The expression:

$$(1.0 + 2.0) * 3.0 / 2.0 ** 2$$

is equal to 2.25, but the expression:

$$(1.0 + 2.0 * 3.0) / 2.0 ** 2$$

is equal to 1.75, and:

$$1.0 + (2.0 * 3.0 / 2.0) ** 2$$

is equal to 10.0. Why? Just do the computations enclosed within the parentheses first, and you should arrive at the same answers.

It is possible to code one set of parentheses within another; this is called *nesting*. For example, the value of:

$$((1.0 + 2.0) * (3.0 / 2.0)) ** 2$$

is the same as:

$$(3.0 \quad * \quad 1.5 \quad) ** 2$$

which is 20.25. Compute the value of the *inner* parentheses first. Most versions of FORTRAN allow for as many as seven levels of parentheses. Check the reference manual for the limit on your system.

It is strongly recommended that you use parentheses when writing arithmetic expressions. Consider, for example, the expression:

$$3.1416 * (RADIUS ** 2)$$

Are the parentheses needed? No. Exponentiation would be done first even if they had not been coded. The parentheses, however, do not hurt, and the intent of the programmer is much more clearly indicated than it would have been had they not been used. *When in doubt, parenthesize.*

Occasionally, parentheses *must* be used. For example, the expression:

$$X * -4.0$$

is illegal; it should be written as:

$$X * (-4.0)$$

Under most versions of FORTRAN, you cannot code two successive operators unless they are separated by a left parenthesis.

You may have noticed that, in the examples cited above, variables, constants, and operators were separated by spaces (blank characters). Blank spaces are not required by FORTRAN; in fact, they may be ignored by your compiler. They were coded for the convenience of the programmer, simply to make the expression easier to read.

Any expression that includes both real and integer values is called a *mixed mode* expression. Great care must be taken in coding such expressions. Consider, for example:

$$5.5 + 2 / 8$$

Given the hierarchy of FORTRAN, the answer should be obvious: 2 divided by 8 is 0.25, and 5.5 plus 0.25 is 5.75. FORTRAN would *not* arrive at that answer. In FORTRAN, the division would be done first, as expected. However, both 2 and 8 are integers, so the intermediate result would be integer. An integer number has no decimal part. What is 0.25 equal to if you throw away the decimal part? Zero! The value of 2 / 8 is zero. The value of 2.0 / 8.0 is, however, 0.25. Do you see the difference? FORTRAN performs arithmetic operations one at a time. If both values are integer, the intermediate result is integer; if both values are real, the result is real.

What if the two values are mixed? What, for example, is the value of 2.0 / 8? The answer is 0.25. If one of the values is real, the answer is real; real takes precedence.

Do not rely on the computer to make the right choice for you. If you mean real, code the decimal point; if you mean integer, don't code a decimal point. You may get away with sloppy code, but eventually it will catch up with you.

One final comment before we leave this topic. When raising a number to a power, should the exponent be real or integer? If the operation calls for raising the number to a fractional power, the answer is obvious, but what about squaring or cubing a number? Should you code X ** 3 or X * 3.0? On most computer systems, an integer exponent is far more efficient and generates a somewhat more accurate answer than does a real exponent. Use integer powers whenever possible.

EXERCISES

1. Write FORTRAN expressions for the following algebraic expressions:

    a. x+y+2z+8

    b. 2a + 4b + 4c - 2d

    c. $\dfrac{x + y}{a + b}$

    d. $\dfrac{-b + \sqrt{b^2 - 4ac}}{2a}$

e. $xy - 2x^2 y^2 + 3x^3 y^3$

f. $\dfrac{a}{3} + \dfrac{b}{4}^2 - \dfrac{c}{3}^3$

g. abcd/wxyz + 18.5

Note that each algebraic variable is a single letter.

2. Find, and code in FORTRAN, formulas for the following:

    a. The area of a triangle.

    b. The volume of a cube.

    c. The volume of a sphere.

    d. The volume of a right circular cylinder.

    e. A baseball player's batting average.

    f. A baseball pitcher's earned run average.

    g. A grade point average.

    h. The interest earned on a savings account (assume 5% interest).

3. Given that A = 1.0, B = 2.0, C = 3.0, I = 1, J = 2, and K = 3, find the values of the following FORTRAN expressions:

    a. A + B/4.0 + C

    b. I + J/4 + K

    c. (A + B) * (C + 2.0) / B

    d. (I + J + K) / 3

    e. B ** J * C

    f. I + J + K ** 2

    g. (A + B + C) ** 2

    h. I + K / J + J

    i. A + C / B + B

    j. (I + J) / (I + K)

ASSIGNMENT STATEMENTS

Assignment statements are used to assign the value of an expression to a variable; for example:

AREA = 3.1416 * (RADIUS ** 2)

Do *not* code

8 = A

or

3.1416 * (RADIUS ** 2) = AREA

A single variable must be coded to the left of the equal sign.

The equal sign in an assignment statement may not mean exactly what you think it does. Consider, for example, the statement:

K = K + 1

Clearly, equating K to K + 1 is a violation of the rules of algebra. A better interpretation of the FORTRAN statement shown above is: Assign the value of the expression K + 1 to the variable named K. It is legal and quite common in FORTRAN.

The assignment statement is FORTRAN's data manipulation statement. All computational logic is specified through the assignment statement. In a typical FORTRAN program, you will construct a loop that begins with a READ statement. Once a record has been read, the data will be manipulated by a series of assignment statements. The loop ends with a WRITE statement, sending the results of your computations out to the printer or the terminal. A GO TO or IF statement following the WRITE sends control back to the top so that the loop can be repeated.

CONDITIONAL STATEMENTS

An assignment statement, a READ statement, and a WRITE statement are *unconditional*; when such statements are encountered, they will always be executed. A GO TO statement is an unconditional branch; if the statement says GO TO 10, control will always be transferred to statement number 10. An IF statement is different. The action taken in response to an IF is dependent upon a condition.

Consider, for example, an IF. . .THEN. . .ELSE logical structure. The general form of such a structure is:

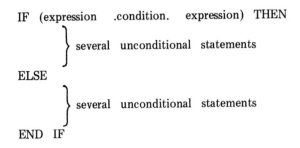

IF (expression   .condition.   expression) THEN

} several unconditional statements

ELSE

} several unconditional statements

END IF

First, a condition is tested. If the condition is true, the statements following the word THEN are executed, and the statements following the word ELSE are not executed. If the condition is false, the opposite happens: the THEN logic is skipped and the ELSE logic is executed. Do you see why the IF statement is called *conditional*?

Conditions

In FORTRAN, the condition to be tested is enclosed in a set of parentheses, and follows the word IF. The general structure of the conditional is:

(expression   .condition.   expression)

Essentially, two expressions are compared. The condition can be any of the following:

FORTRAN code	Meaning
.EQ.	equal to
.GT.	greater than
.LT.	less than
.GE.	greater than or equal to
.LE.	less than or equal to
.NE.	not equal to

In some versions of FORTRAN, the mathematical symbols $=$, $>$, and $<$ can be used.

For example, consider the conditional:

(COUNT   .LE.   100.0)

Read it as follows: COUNT is less than or equal to 100.0. That statement is either true (COUNT really is less than or equal to 100.0), or it is false. The action to be taken depends on the condition.

Generally, the programmer will compare a variable to a constant or a variable to another variable; for example,

(NUMBER   .LT.   25)

or: (VALUE   .GT.   UPLIM)

or: (TEST   .EQ.   0.0)

Avoid mixed mode comparisons; in other words, do not compare an integer and a real number. Such comparisons will work; FORTRAN simply converts the integer value to real and does the comparison. The results can, however, be just a bit inaccurate, and even if the accuracy problem is not a concern, why force the computer to do the extra work of converting the data from one form to another?

You should also be very careful of .EQ. comparisons, particularly on real numbers. The statement:

IF (X   .EQ.   0.0)

is true *only* if X is *exactly* equal to 0.0. A very small number such as .1E–70 is *not* exactly equal to 0.0; if this were the value of X, the condition would be false. Whenever possible, use .GE. or .LE. rather than .EQ.

A final comment: The statement

IF (X + Y   .LT.   A * B) etc.

is legal; two *expressions* are compared. For clarity, most programmers stay with comparisons that involve simple variables and simple constants; it is easier to follow such logic. *Any* two expressions can be compared, however; just be careful.

The IF. . .THEN. . .ELSE Block

IF. . .THEN. . .ELSE logic has already been introduced. A condition is tested. If the condition is true, one block of instructions (assignment statements, READs, WRITES, and/or GO TOs) is executed. If the condition is false, a different block of statements gets control. The IF. . .THEN. . .ELSE has been widely accepted as the programmer's standard conditional logic block. It has been included in the latest ANSI FORTRAN standard, FORTRAN 77.

Not all versions of FORTRAN include an IF. . .THEN. . .ELSE block; many existing FORTRAN compilers are based on the 1966 standard. On your system, you may have to use a simple *logical IF* or an *arithmetic IF*.

The Logical IF

A logical IF statement resembles the first part of an IF. . .THEN. . .ELSE block. The general form of a logical IF is:

```
IF  (expression  .condition.  expression)  statement
```

Once again, two expressions are compared. If the condition is true, the *single statement* following the condition is executed; if the condition is not true, the statement is not executed.

For example, you might code:

IF (NUMBER .GE. 0) N = N + 1

If the value of NUMBER is in fact greater than or equal to 0, the statement N = N + 1 will be executed. If the value of NUMBER is negative, the statement is *not* executed.

Most versions of FORTRAN allow the programmer to code any unconditional statement in the logical IF—an assignment statement, a REAL, a WRITE, or a GO TO. Others are not so flexible, allowing only a GO TO to be coded. Check the reference manual or ask your instructor for the restrictions of your system.

The logical IF can be viewed as a special case of IF. . .THEN. . .ELSE logic. Only the THEN block is coded, and this block is restricted to a single statement. Such simple logical structures are not uncommon.

The Arithmetic IF

Early versions of FORTRAN used an arithmetic IF. The general form of this instruction is:

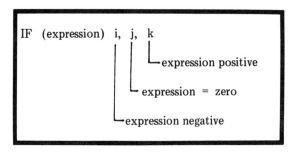

where i, j, and k are statement numbers. If the expression is negative, the IF is equivalent to GO TO i. If the expression is equal to zero, the statement is equivalent to GO TO j. If it is positive, a functionally equivalent statement would be GO TO k.

We will not be using the arithemtic IF in this text.

EXERCISES

If you have not already done so, return to Chapter 2, page 36, and begin writing some programs.

3

Branching
and Looping:
Simple Loops

OVERVIEW

There is an elementary truism in the field of computer programming: The only way to learn to program is to program. We have covered many of the elements of the FORTRAN language; now it is time to put our knowledge to work. In this chapter, we will plan and code two programs, each involving repetitive logic—a loop. One program will compute the sum of a series of integers. The second will generate a metric-to-English conversion table. Two new FORTRAN features will be introduced: the DO loop and the FORMAT statement.

61

LOOPS

It makes very little sense to write a computer program to find the area of a single circle or the average of a half dozen numbers. Programming takes time. Frankly, it is easier to solve a small problem on a pocket calculator than to write a program to solve it.

Why then do we write programs? Not all problems are small. Although the calculator is fine for computing the area of a single circle, a person assigned the task of computing the areas of all circles with integer radii ranging from 1 to 1000 centemeters would soon grow tired of pushing buttons. When a set of logic, even simple logic, must be repeated many times, it makes sense to take the time to carefully define that logic once, in the form of a computer program. Given a program, it is possible to instruct the computer to execute the logic over and over again, automatically. This is the real advantage of the computer. Repetitive logic need be defined only *once*. By placing this logic in a **loop**, it can be executed as often as necessary.

Most programs involve setting up one or more loops. A loop is a set or series of instructions. It has a clearly defined beginning and a clearly defined end; for example, in the average program, the loop began with a READ statement and ended with a GO TO. The idea is simple. Start at the beginning, execute the instructions in the loop in sequence, and then go back to the beginning and do it again.

The idea of repetitive logic, however, is not the whole story. Consider, for example, the following loop:

70   N = N + 1

GO TO 70

Clearly something is missing. It is possible to enter the loop by executing statement number 70, but once in, there is no way out! This is called an endless loop, and it's a common beginner's error.

To be valid, every loop must have an exit, a way out. There are many different ways to construct a loop exit. In the average problem, we tested for an end of data condition, exiting the loop when the input value was negative. As an alternative, if the number of times a loop must be repeated is known, we can simply count, leaving the loop when the counter reaches the critical value. Consider instead a problem in which the objective is to find some critical value; for example, how many integers must we add until the sum exceeds 1000? Here, the loop will be executed until the critical value is reached.

In this chapter, we'll be writing two programs, each involving a loop that is controlled by a counter. In Chapter 4, two programs requiring somewhat more complex loop structures will be coded.

A "COUNT" LOOP: THE SUM OF A SERIES OF INTEGERS

What is the sum of the integers from 1 to 200? More generally, what is the sum of the integers from 1 to some unknown upper limit, N? In an algebra course, you may have been exposed to a formula for computing this sum directly. A program using this formula will be more efficient (better!) than a program that sets up a loop to sum the integers, but, for purposes of illustration, we are going to set up a loop anyway.

Ignoring the formula, how would you go about finding the sum of a series of integers? You might begin with a very simple example. If N = 5, the sum of the integers from 1 to N is 1 + 2 + 3 + 4 + 5. Adding two terms at a time generates the following accumulations: 1 + 2 is 3; 3 + 3 is 6; 6 + 4 is 10; 10 + 5 is 15. The sum of the integers from 1 to 5 is 15. A few more simple examples should establish the pattern.

Now, it's time to define the logic. Essentially, finding the sum of a series of integers involves counting and adding. The key steps are:

1. Add the counter to the accumulator.

2. Add 1 to the counter.

3. If the counter is less than or equal to the limit, N, repeat the first two steps.

What about the initial values? What is N? Where should we start the counter and the accumulator? We are, after all, trying to develop a computer program, and we know that the computer assumes nothing; thus, we might define:

1. Initialize N, the upper limit.

2. Initialize the accumulator to zero.

3. Initialize the counter to 1.

Now the main program loop can be entered:

4. Add the counter to the accumulator.

5. Add 1 to the counter.

6. Is the counter less than or equal to N?

7. If yes, go back to statement number 4.

What happens after the loop has been executed the desired number of times? We are ready to print our results and end the program, thus:

8. Print N and the accumulated sum.

9. Stop.

Putting all these steps together, we can now draw the flowchart of Fig. 3.1.

What variables will we need? First, we'll need a variable to hold the upper limit; let's call that N. A counter will be needed; K will do nicely. Finally, an accumulator, ISUM, will be needed to hold the sum of the integers. Note that all the variables are integer variables. Our planning is now complete; the FORTRAN program can be written.

Incidentially, before we continue, you should know that the program we have planned is not the *only* possible solution to this problem. Earlier, we discussed using a simple equation to find the sum of a series of integers, and that algorithm would certainly represent an excellent way to solve this problem. We might choose to control our loop differently, too. Why not, for example, start the counter at N and *subtract* 1 each time through the loop until the counter reaches zero? Other, equally valid solutions are possible.

Writing the "Integers" Program in FORTRAN

We already know all the instructions we need to write this program. The first three logic blocks can be coded as:

```
READ  (5,*)  N

ISUM = 0

K = 1
```

Next, the loop can be written. It's a very simple loop, consisting of only three instructions:

```
10    ISUM = ISUM + K

      K = K + 1

      IF (K  .LE.  N)  GO TO 10
```

Finally, the output can be obtained and the program ended:

```
WRITE  (6,*)  N,ISAM

STOP

END
```

That's about it. Once the planning is finished, coding is (and should be) relatively simple.

There is, however, one more point to consider before we leave this program. The loop coded above essentially counts from 1 to some upper limit, exiting the loop when this limit is reached. This sequence is so common in programming, that most languages

Fig. 3.1: *Flowchart for a program to compute the sum of the integers from 1 to N.*

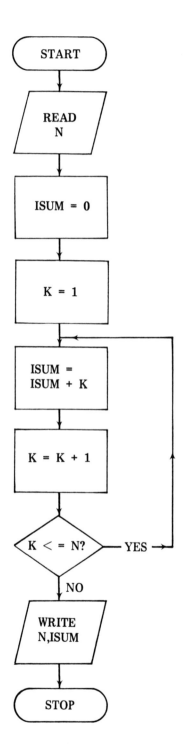

Fig. 3.2: *A comparison of two equivalent loop structures.*

the old way	with a DO loop
K = 1	DO 50 K = 1,N
10 ISUM = ISUM + K	ISUM = ISUM + K
K = K + 1	50 CONTINUE
IF (K .LE. N) GO TO 10	

contain special instructions to simplify the coding of such loops. FORTRAN is no exception. In FORTRAN, a simple "count" loop can be defined by coding a DO loop.

Fig. 3.2 shows the loop we just coded on the left and an equivalent DO loop on the right. The DO statement defines the top of the loop; the CONTINUE statement defines the bottom. As the loop begins, the control variable, in this case, K, is set equal to the initial value (1 in this example). The instructions contained in the loop are then executed. When the end of the loop is encountered, the control variable, K, is incremented by 1. If K is less than or equal to the upper limit, N, logic returns to the top of the loop; if not, control passes to the first statement following the loop.

Let's put it another way. The statement:

DO 50 K = 1,N

really means: DO (or repeat) all the statements down to and including statement number 50, varying the value of K from an initial 1 to a maximum of "N". The general form of a DO loop is:

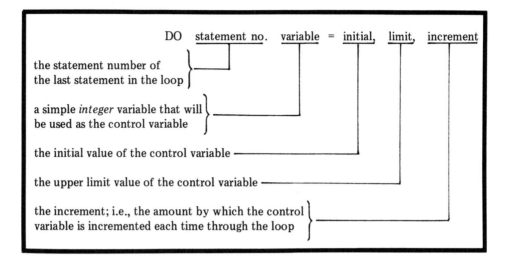

DO statement no. variable = initial, limit, increment

the statement number of
the last statement in the loop

a simple *integer* variable that will
be used as the control variable

the initial value of the control variable

the upper limit value of the control variable

the increment; i.e., the amount by which the control
variable is incremented each time through the loop

Note that the control variable *must* be integer, and the initial value, limit, and increment must *all* be integer variables or constants.

What is the difference between the two loops of Fig. 3.2? Obviously, the DO loop requires one less instruction, but that is only a surface difference. Without the DO structure, we coded the instructions to initialize, increment, and test the control variable, along with the other instructions in the loop. Most of our code was concerned with controlling the loop, and *not* with performing the primary function of the loop, adding K to ISUM. With the DO structure, the loop controls are implied. In effect, the DO statement defines the start of the loop and the CONTINUE statement defines the end of the loop. We can concentrate on what the loop is really designed to do; the loop controls do not "clutter" our logic. That is the big advantage of DO loops.

A version of the integer program using a DO loop is shown in Fig. 3.3. Note that the "increment" portion of the DO statement is missing; if the increment is 1, it need not be coded.

The Logic of a DO Loop

What exactly does this program do? It is often very instructive to "play computer" on a simple program like this. By following step by step the computer's reaction to the program statements, it is possible to gain a much better understanding of what the program really means. The steps actually executed by this program for an input value N = 3 are outlined in Fig. 3.4. Use a card or a ruler to underline the "current step" as you follow the program logic.

The first step in the program is to input a value for N. Space is set aside to hold this value, and a data card is read, or the programmer is asked to type the number on the terminal. As the value is read into the program, it is stored in memory. Note that the values of other variables are still unknown.

The next instruction initializes ISUM, the accumulator. Main memory space is set aside to hold this field, and is initialized to zero.

The loop comes next. First, the control variable, is initialized to 1 (Fig. 3.4, line 3). Following initialization, the assignment statement is executed; variable ISUM is now equal to 1. The final step in the first iteration of the loop, identified logically as the CONTINUE statement, increments the control variable by 1. Note in Fig. 3.4 (line 5) that K is now equal to 2.

Is K greater than N, the upper limit? K is 2; N is 3; the answer is clearly "no". Thus control returns to the top of the loop, and K is once again added to ISUM (Fig. 3.4, line 6); ISUM is now 3. The control variable is incremented again, and the condition $(K > N)$ is tested. K is 3; N is 3; once again the condition is false. As a result, the loop is repeated yet another time.

The assignment statement is executed (Fig. 3.4, line 8). K is incremented (line 9). K now exceeds N; therefore the loop ends. The final instruction executed by the program is the WRITE statement, which sends whatever is in N and whatever is in ISUM to the printer.

Take the time to follow the program logic described above. Understand this example, it is important. If you can follow the logic, you will know what the computer does. If you know what the computer does, you will find it easier to write future programs.

The increment in this loop is 1. What if an increment other than 1 was desired? What if, for example, the problem asked the programmer to find the sum of all the odd integers, 1, 3, 5, 7, . . ., up to some limit, N? The statement:

```
DO  25  I = 1,N,2
```

might provide control. What if the increment were subject to change; in other words, what if we wanted the program to sometimes work with increments of 1, sometimes 2, sometimes 3, and so on? We might code:

```
READ  (5,*)  LIMIT,  INC

DO  100  K = 1,LIMIT,INC
```

followed by additional instructions.

The initial value can be either an integer constant or an integer variable. It doesn't have to be 1, either. For example:

Fig. 3.3: *The integer program using a DO loop.*

```
C
C
C                                    *  PROGRAM TO COMPUTE THE SUM OF
C                                    *  THE INTEGERS FROM 1 TO AN
C                                    *  UNKNOWN LIMIT, N.
C                                    *     WRITTEN BY:  W.S. DAVIS
C                                    *                   1/10/81
                                     *  *  *  *  *  *  *  *  *  *  *  *  *  *  *
        READ (5,*) N
        ISUM = 0
        DO 50 K=1,N
           ISUM = ISUM + K
     50 CONTINUE
        WRITE (6,*) N,ISUM
        STOP
        END
```

Fig. 3.4: *The step by step execution of the integer program.*

Instruction	N	ISUM	K
1. READ N	3	?	?
2. ISUM = 0	3	0	?
3. K=1	3	0	1
4. ISUM = ISUM + K	3	1	1
5. K = K + 1	3	1	2
6. ISUM = ISUM + K	3	3	2
7. K = K + 1	3	3	3
8. ISUM = ISUM + K	3	6	3
9. K = K + 1	3	6	4
10. K now exceeds N; terminate			
11. WRITE N, ISUM			

the loop

to printer

3   6

$$DO \quad 40 \quad I = 10,200,5$$

is perfectly valid.

In the DO loops coded above, a CONTINUE statement was used to mark the end of the loop. This is not necessary; any READ, WRITE, or assignment statement can be the last statement in the loop. Using a CONTINUE statement is, however, a good idea, as the DO and the CONTINUE clearly mark the loop's boundaries.

ANOTHER COUNT LOOP: A METRIC-TO-ENGLISH CONVERSION TABLE

The United States is gradually converting to the metric system. Over the next several years, we will encounter measurements in both systems, so a conversion from metric-to-English or from English-to-metric will often be necessary. To aid in this conversion, we would like to generate a table showing distances ranging from 1 to 100 kilometers along with the equivalent measurements in feet and miles.

Where do we start? Our first step should be to define the algorithms or conversion factors. One kilometer is equal to how many miles? How many feet? How can we find out? You probably have a science book that contains conversion factors. If not, try a good dictionary. Almost invariably, by looking up the term "meter", you can find a conversion expressing the length of a meter in either feet, or inches, or both. A meter is equivalent to 3.281 feet. A kilometer is simply 1000 meters; if one meter is equal to 3.281 feet, 1000 meters is equal to 3281 feet.

A similar set of computations can be used to develop a factor to convert kilometers to miles. The dictionary tells us that there are 5280 feet per mile. If a kilometer is equal to 3281 feet, then a kilometer must be equal to 3281 feet divided by 5280 feet/mile, which is 0.6214 miles. We now have our two conversion factors, and can compute a few key table values, as follows:

KILOMETERS	FEET	MILES
1	3281	0.6214
50	164,050	31.0700
100	328,100	62.1400

Later, this skeleton table will prove useful in checking our results.

What next? Having defined our conversion factors, we might turn our attention to the variables to be manipulated by our program. We'll need one to represent kilometers—KILO seems logical. Miles will be represented by MILES; feet, by FEET.

Finally, we can define the program logic. Essentially, this program will involve a single loop. The number of kilometers will be initialized to 1. The equivalent number of feet and miles will be computed using the conversion factors developed above;

70

then the values of KILO, FEET, and MILES will be printed. The number of kilometers will be incremented by 1, and the cycle repeated until KILO is greater than 100. A flowchart of this logic is shown as Fig. 3.5.

We are not quite ready to begin writing the code, however. Consider the partial table that was prepared a few paragraphs back. The computed values are nicely arranged in columns, with a descriptive header at the top of each column. Where did these headers come from? How did we manage to align the headers and the data?

The table shown earlier was produced on a typewriter. Basically, we started by typing the headers, using reasonable spacing between the words. We then carefully aligned the data under the headers to form columns, essentially by counting print positions. The FORTRAN programmer can cause the printer to do much the same thing by using a FORMAT statement along with a WRITE statement.

A FORMAT statement is used to provide a position by position description of an output (or input) record. Each character, be it a letter, a digit, a punctuation mark, or a blank, occupies one print position. The FORMAT statement allows the programmer to specify the exact content of the line.

Consider, for example, the column headers:

KILOMETERS   FEET   MILES

Assume that we want KILOMETERS to start in position 5, FEET to begin in print position 20, and MILES in position 30. The two statements:

WRITE (6,11)

11 FORMAT (T5, 'KILOMETERS' ,T20, 'FEET' ,T30, 'MILES')

would achieve this objective. Let's take a close look at these instructions.

The WRITE instruction is unusual in that it lists no variables. There are no variables to be printed in this line; the column headers are constant. Since no variables are to be printed, none are listed.

Following the key word WRITE, enclosed within the parentheses, are two numbers. The 6 identifies the output device; nothing new here. The second number, the 11, is the number of a FORMAT statement.

Now, on to the FORMAT statement itself. Look inside the parentheses. The first thing you see is T5. This is a tab **FORMAT** item; it is much like the tab key on a typewriter. T5 means tab (or skip) over to position number 5. Next comes the word KILOMETERS enclosed between a set of apostrophes (or single quote marks). This is a literal constant; in effect, the printer will be asked to print "literally", whatever is between the apostrophes. Following the first literal is another tab item—T20. It indicates that the printer is to skip to position 20 before printing the next header, which is another literal constant, 'FEET'. Finally, T30 skips to position 30, and the literal 'MILES' is printed starting with this position. Note that the individual FORMAT items are separated by commas. Do you see how the format of the header line can be precisely controlled?

Within the main loop of the program (Fig. 3.5), a table of values for kilometers, feet, and miles is to be printed. We would like to align the values under the appropriate headers. The word "KILOMETERS" is 10 characters long; the biggest value for kilometers in the table will be 100, a 3-digit number. The header started in position 5 (a tab FORMAT). If we start the values in position 9 (T9), the numbers will be nicely aligned under the header. A similar argument can be advanced for each of the table columns; by carefully matching the tab items on a header and its related values, easy-to-read columns can be prepared.

What about the data values themselves? When FORMAT statements are used, each variable listed in a READ or a WRITE statement must be accompanied by an individual FORMAT item. Consider, for example, the values of the variable KILO. KILO is integer; thus the values to be printed will be integer. An integer value is described with an I-type FORMAT item. For example, we might code the following two statements:

WRITE (6,12) KILO

12 FORMAT (I3)

The first variable listed is KILO; the first FORMAT item is of integer type. The number 3 indicates the number of positions to be allocated to the value of KILO—it's a 3-digit number.

What if more than one variable is to be output? For example:

WRITE (6,25) N1,N2,N3

25 FORMAT (I5,I7,I1)

Match the variable to the FORMAT item. The first variable is N1; the first FORMAT item is an I5; N1 is (at most) a 5-digit number. N2 is the second variable; I7 is the second FORMAT item; N2 is a 7-digit number. The last variable listed is N3. The last FORMAT item is an I1. N3 is a 1-digit number.

Real variables call for a different type of FORMAT item. A real variable can (in fact, does) have a decimal point; integers do not. The decimal point takes up a print position, just like a digit does. Also, we are concerned not only with the number of positions or characters to be output, but also with the number of digits to the right of the decimal point.

The most commonly used FORMAT item for a real variable is the F-type FORMAT item. In general, it is coded as

Fig. 3.5: *A flowchart of the metric conversion table program.*

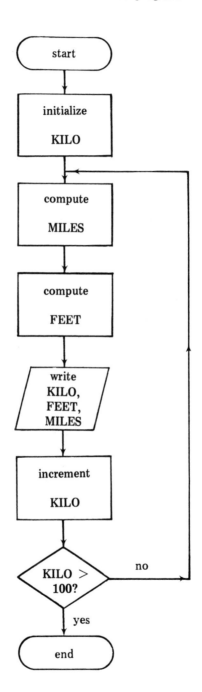

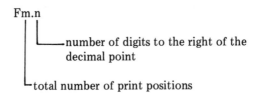

Fm.n
└── number of digits to the right of the decimal point
└── total number of print positions

For example, the maximum value for miles in the partial table developed earlier was 62.1400. A total of seven print positions are needed to hold this number—six digits plus the decimal point. Four digits appear to the right of the decimal point. The FORMAT item to describe this field would be: F7.4. Just to be on the safe side, we might use F8.4, although it really isn't necessary.

Remember the FORMAT statement we used to describe the column headers? It was:

```
11  FORMAT  (T5, 'KILOMETERS' ,T20, 'FEET' ,T30, 'MILES')
```

In the program, we will be writing values of KILO, FEET, and MILES. If the statement:

```
12  FORMAT  (T9,I3,T20,F8.0,T30,F8.4)
```

is used with this WRITE statement, can you see how the column headers and the data values will be aligned?

One final point before we move on. A well-designed report or table generally has column headers begin at the top of a page. How can the programmer cause headers to start at the top of a new page? The answer to this question depends on the computer system or printer used. Generally, however, it's a pretty simple task. The first position in the output line is used as a carriage control character, and serves to control printer spacing. A carriage control character equal to 1 means "skip to the top of the next page"; a blank means "skip one line and print". To put the value "1" in the first position of an output line, simply code a literal constant '1' as the first item in the FORMAT statement; for example:

```
11  FORMAT  ('1' ,T5, 'KILOMETERS' ,T20, 'FEET' ,T30, 'MILES')
```

For single spacing, you can code a blank character ('   ') as the first FORMAT item, or simply tab past position 1, thus making certain that nothing is printed there—FORTRAN will add the blank.

Additional details on the FORMAT statement can be found in Module B, immediately following this chapter.

Now we can write the FORTRAN program (Fig. 3.6) using FORMAT statements. You should have little trouble following the logic.

Fig. 3.6: *The conversion table program.*

```
C                                    *  PROGRAM TO CONVERT KILOMETERS
C                                    *  TO FEET AND MILES.
C                                    *    WRITTEN BY:  W.S. DAVIS
C                                    *            1/10/81
C                                    * * * * * * * * * * * * * * *
          REAL MILES
          WRITE (6,11)
          DO 50 KILO = 1,100
              MILES = KILO * 0.6214
              FEET = KILO * 3281.0
              WRITE (6,12) KILO,FEET,MILES
       50 CONTINUE
          STOP
       11 FORMAT ('1',T5,'KILOMETERS',T20,'FEET',T30,'MILES')
       12 FORMAT (T9,I3,T20,F8.0,T30,F8.4)
          END
```

Note the first statement in the program:

REAL MILES

Why is it necessary? MILES begins with the letter "M"; thus it is (by default) an integer variable. We want MILES to hold a real number. We could have used RMILES, but this variable name would not have described the statistic as well as MILES. The explicit type statement overrides the default; MILES is now a real variable.

Note that all the FORMAT statements have been gathered together and grouped at the end of the program (between the STOP and END statements). A FORMAT statement is *not* an executable statement. A FORMAT statement *describes* data. Statements like READ, WRITE, GO TO, and assignment statements *do things* to data. Do you sense the difference? Since a FORMAT statement merely describes data, it can be placed anywhere in the program. It is a good idea, however, to place these statements at the end (or the beginning) of the program, so they don't get in the way of someone who might want to read the program (like you or your instructor). Note also that you *cannot* GO TO a FORMAT statement or use one as the last statement in a DO loop.

SUMMARY

In this chapter we wrote two programs, both involving count-controlled loops. The first program was designed to compute the sum of the integers from 1 to an unknown upper limit, N. A solution was carefully planned, flowcharted, and then coded. A count loop is very common in programming. FORTRAN includes a DO loop structure to make the coding of such loops easier. We introduced the DO loop and then recoded the integer problem using this structure. Finally, we followed an imaginary computer step by step as it executed the program.

A second program called for the creation of a metric-to-English conversion table, comparing kilometers with feet and miles. First, the algorithms were developed and a solution to the problem was planned; then the FORTRAN code was written. The only new FORTRAN feature was the FORMAT statement, which allowed us to instruct the program to print the table in neat columns, complete with column headers.

EXERCISES

1. Write a program to compute and print the areas of a series of circles with radii ranging from 1 to 25 in increments of 1.

2. In Chapter 1, problem number 8, you were asked to develop a flowchart for a program to generate a temperature conversion table. Write this program now.

3. Chapter 1, exercise 6, presented another problem that you can now code. If an individual is paid 1 cent today, 2 cents tomorrow, 4 cents the day after, and so on (the amount doubles each day), how much money would that person have after 30 days?

4. Since 1 kilometer equals 1093.6 yards and 0.5396 nautical miles, add these two computations to the distance table program developed in the text. The program should list kilometers, feet, miles, yards, and nautical miles for each value of kilometers from 1 to 100.

5. The factorial of an integer is defined as the product of that integer and all positive integers less than it. For example,

$$10! = 10 \times 9 \times 8 \times 7 \times 6 \times 5 \times 4 \times 3 \times 2 \times 1$$

and $4! = 4 \times 3 \times 2 \times 1$

By definition, $1! = 1$ and $0! = 0$. Write a program to compute and print the factorial of an unknown integer; in other words, input the integer, compute its factorial, and print the answer.

6. Assume that an amount of money invested in a savings account earns interest at an annual rate of $5\frac{1}{2}$ percent. The amount of money would represent a beginning balance. The interest earned during the first year would be $5\frac{1}{2}\%$ of this figure. The ending balance would be the sum of the beginning balance and the interest earned. As we moved into the second year, this new balance would become the beginning balance for computing the interest earned during the second year. Write a program to read an initial amount invested; then develop a

table showing the beginning balance, interest earned, and ending balance for each of ten years. You might then generalize your program by reading both an interest rate and the number of years, along with the amount to be invested.

7. Input an integer number. Then compute and print the first ten powers of this number. It is possible that, if your number is big enough, your computer system will not be able to compute the tenth power. See if you can discover where this overflow condition occurs.

8. An instructor wants to develop a grade conversion table to help translate hour exam grades into a part of a final grade. The hour exam counts 25 percent of the final grade. If a student scores 100 on the exam, he or she will get 25 grade points. An 80 is worth 20 grade points; a 50 is worth 12.5, and so on. Write a program to develop a list of grade point equivalents for grades ranging from a high of 100 to a low of 40, assuming the 25% grade factor. Now, generalize the program to develop a similar list given any percentage grade factor.

9. Write a program to compute the sum of the integers from an unknown lower limit, L1, to an unknown upper limit, L2.

10. Write a program to compute the sum of the *odd* integers from 1 to an unknown upper limit.

11. On the moon, a human being would weigh 16% of his or her earth weight. On Jupiter, this figure would jump to 264%. On Venus, 85% would be the figure; on Mars, a somewhat smaller planet, you would weigh only 38% of your earth weight. Write a program comparing earth weight to the equivalent weight on each of these planets for weights ranging from 50 pounds to 250 pounds in increments of 10.

12. One technique for computing the depreciation of a piece of equipment or a building is the sum-of-the-years'-digits method. For example, assume that an item is expected to last for 5 years. The sum of the years' digits would be $1 + 2 + 3 + 4 + 5$, which is 15. During the first year, 5/15 of the value of the asset would be depreciated; during the second year, 4/15 would be depreciated, and so on, until, during the fifth year, the remaining 1/15 would be depreciated. Write a program to input the value of an asset and the estimated life of this asset and then print a depreciation schedule showing the amount depreciated for each year of life.

13. Write a program to accumulate the series: $1 + 1/2 + 1/3 + 1/4 + 1/5 + \ldots + 1/100$. Print the answer.

Module B

FORMAT Statements

OVERVIEW

The FORTRAN programmer often has a need to control or describe the precise, character by character contents of an input or output record. FORMAT statements can be used to achieve this objective. In this module, we'll consider some of the FORMAT statement coding rules.

WHAT IS A FORMAT STATEMENT?

A FORMAT statement is simply a description of an input or output record. Other statements—READ, WRITE, GO TO—*do* something. The FORMAT statement merely describes.

FORMAT statements are coded in combination with READ and WRITE statements. The general form of the READ is:

    READ (m,n) list

where "m" is the device number, "n" is a FORMAT statement number, and "list" is a list of variables. The WRITE statement has much the same form:

    WRITE (m,n) list

Very simply, the purpose of the FORMAT statement is to describe the record read by the associated READ statement, or to describe the record written by the associated WRITE statement. That is all the FORMAT statement does.

THE GENERAL FORM OF A FORMAT STATEMENT

In general, a FORMAT statement takes the following form:

    number FORMAT (item-1,item-2,item-3, . . .)

Every FORMAT statement must have a statement number. Given that the only function of a FORMAT statement is to support an associated READ or WRITE, this makes sense. Following the key word FORMAT is a series of FORMAT items or field description items separated by commas. Each variable in the associated READ or WRITE will have a matching FORMAT item. In addition, the programmer can include literal constants, tab items, blank spaces, and other descriptions between the parentheses.

Let's briefly consider some of the more commonly used FORMAT field description items.

The I-type FORMAT Item

The value of an integer variable is written or read under the control of an I-type FORMAT item. The general form is:

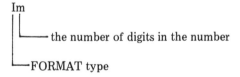

For example, a three-digit integer would call for an I3 FORMAT item, while a seven-digit number would call for I7.

The F-type FORMAT Item

Real numbers have a decimal point. The most commonly used FORMAT item for reading or writing real numbers is the F-type FORMAT. In general code:

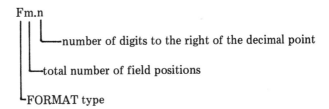

For example, consider a seven digit number with three digits to the right of the decimal point. We have four digits to the left of the decimal point, the point itself, and three digits to the right, a total of eight positions. Thus, a valid FORMAT item would be F8.3. As another example, consider the value "5.". The number consumes two positions—the digit and the decimal point. No digits are found to the right of the decimal point. Can you see why F2.0 would be a reasonable FORMAT?

The E-type FORMAT Item

If you have run programs using unformatted WRITE statements, you may have already seen answers printed in what is called floating point form. For example, the speed of light, 186,000 miles per second, would be printed as 0.186E6, meaning 0.186×10^6. With very large and very small numbers, a programmer may want to use a FORMAT item to control the printing of floating point numbers. This can be done by using an E-type FORMAT. The general form is:

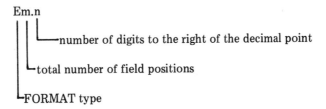

For example, consider the number 0.1234567×10^{25}. We'll use a FORMAT item E12.5. The FORMAT item calls for a total of twelve positions. Five digits are to be to the right of the decimal point. There are seven digits in the number, so two will be to the left of the decimal point. The point itself will be part of the field, as will the letter E. Using this FORMAT, the sample number would be:

12.34567E25

Eleven positions are used; twelve were called for; one position is left for the sign of the number should it be negative.

Tabs

As we saw in Chapter 3, the programmer can use a tab FORMAT to control the spacing of fields across an input or output record. The general form of the tab item is:

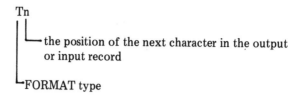

Inserting Blank Spaces

Spaces in an input or output record can be skipped by using an X-type FORMAT item. Simply code the number of spaces to be skipped, followed by the letter X. For example, three spaces can be skipped by coding 3X, and eighteen spaces can be skipped by coding 18X. To skip a single space, type 1X, not just X.

Literal Constants

Literal constants can be added to a FORMAT statement to help identify the output (literals are almost never used on input). A literal constant is simply a string of characters enclosed within a set of apostrophes or single quote marks; for example:

'THIS IS A LITERAL CONSTANT'

Any character found on your keypunch or terminal keyboard can be used as part of a literal constant. The only problem is the apostrophe itself. Apostrophes are used to mark the beginning and the end of a literal constant; thus it should be apparent that including one within the constant could cause trouble. If you must code an apostrophe within a literal constant, code two of them, as in:

' IT' 'S LEGAL TO USE AN APOSTROPHE IF TWO ARE CODED'

Other FORMAT Items

Numerous other types of FORMAT items are available in FORTRAN. We won't describe them here, but as your programming skill increases, you may have need for them. Check your system's reference manual.

Some Examples

Assume that your program is to read the following records:

Positions	Contents
1-5	a 5-digit integer
6-7	blank
8-12	a real number with two digits to the right of the decimal point.

We might use the following two statements to read this record:

        READ (5,25) K,A

    25 FORMAT (I5,2X,F5.2)

FORMAT items are matched with the variables in the list in the order coded—the I5 goes with the variable K, and the F5.2 goes with the variable X. Note that the variable type and the FORMAT type match; they must. The first five positions of the input record are assigned to the variable K. The 2X FORMAT item causes the next two positions (6 and 7) to be skipped. The next five positions (8-12) are then assigned to A, with two digits to the right of the decimal point.

What if an input card is punched with the following format:

Positions	Contents
1-4	an integer number
5	blank
6-9	an integer number
10	blank

and so on, with a series of sixteen 4-digit numbers separated by blanks? How would you write a FORMAT statement? The card contains sixteen numbers. One valid FORMAT statement would be:

    35 FORMAT (I4,1X,I4,1X,I4,1X, . . .)

with the "I4,1X" pattern repeated sixteen times. As an alternative, you might code:

    35 FORMAT (16(I4,1X))

The number 16 is a *repeat factor*. It indicates that the FORMAT items enclosed in the inner parentheses are to be repeated sixteen times. Using a repeat factor can save a great deal of coding. Incidently, the number coded in front of the X-type FORMAT item is really a repeat factor.

What if the FORMAT statement includes too few FORMAT items. For example, what would happen if you coded:

83

READ (5,16) X,Y,Z

16 FORMAT (F7.2)

A value will be read for each item in the list. The F7.2 will be used to read a value for X, but there are no more FORMAT items. When the program reaches the end of the FORMAT statement, it simply returns to the beginning and starts over again, with a new record. In other words, X would be found in the first seven positions of the first record, Y in the first seven positions of the second record, and Z in the first seven positions of the third.

What if the programmer provides too many FORMAT items. For example:

WRITE (6,45) AVG

45 FORMAT (T6, 'AVERAGE = ' ,F5.3,I2)

There is no variable to associate with the I2. This is *not* good coding form. Some versions of FORTRAN will flag this as an error; others will simply ignore the unnecessary FORMAT items. Don't do it. Control your code. Know what you are coding, and why you are coding it.

SOME INPUT POINTERS

Assume that your program is about to execute the following READ instruction:

READ (5,14) NUMBER

14 FORMAT (I5)

The variable NUMBER is clearly a five-digit integer. What if you want to input the value 5? Should the digit 5 be typed in the first position or in the fifth?

Since the FORMAT item is I5, the first five positions in the input record will be associated with the variable. In FORTRAN, on input, *blanks are replaced by zeros.* What is the difference between 00005 and 50000? When using FORMAT-controlled input, the programmer *must* remember to *right justify* numbers. Four zeros followed by the digit 5 would be correct, given the I5 FORMAT. Four blanks followed by a 5 would also be correct. The digit 5 followed by four blanks is wrong, unless you mean to enter the value 50,000.

When entering real numbers, do you or do you not type the decimal point? You can do it either way. For example, assume we have the FORMAT item F5.2. Five input positions will be assigned to the associated variable. If you type the decimal point, the computer will (internally) place it where you indicate. If you do not type the decimal point, the computer will assume it. For example, if your input record contains 12345 in these five positions, and if the FORMAT is F5.2, two digits will be assumed to the right of the decimal point—the value would be 123.45.

What if you fail to right justify your number? Assume a FORMAT of F7.3. Type the digits 123 in the first three positions of this field, leaving the last four blank. Remember that blanks are zeros. What you really have is 1230000; assuming three digits to the right of the decimal point, the value is 1230.000, which is probably not correct. What if the decimal point is typed—123.0, for example? Now, the actual decimal point takes control. The seven field positions will be 123.000, but the decimal point is where you want it.

Finally, how do you indicate the sign of an input number? Just type it; for example, –10, or – 12.52. Normally, the plus sign is not entered; a number without a sign is assumed to be positive.

The professional programmer often must process data that has been prepared by a keypunch operator or data entry clerk, usually to a precise format. Thus, formatted input is necessary. On most of your programs, however, you will find unformatted input much easier. Unless the application calls for FORMAT control of input, use the unformatted READ.

SOME OUTPUT POINTERS

FORMAT statements are almost always used with output. Well-formatted output, complete with literal explanations of the results of a program, are easy to understand. The intent of the program is to produce output that some human being can interpret. Good FORMAT control simplifies understanding.

One common problem faced by the programmer is printer control. This is not a concern on a program that prints a single value as output, but when tables or lengthy reports are generated, the ability to print headers at the top of each new page is most useful. In most versions of FORTRAN, the programmer can control printer spacing by controlling the first character of the output line. Simply code a single-character literal constant as the first FORMAT item. The following standard spacing codes are normally used:

Code	Meaning
blank	single space—skip one line and print
zero	double space—skip two lines and print
1	skip to the top of the next page
+	do not skip—overprint

Overprinting might be used to underline a header. For example, consider the following instructions:

```
WRITE  (6,11)

WRITE  (6.12)

11  FORMAT  ('1' ,T10, 'ID NUMBER' ,T25, 'SCORE')

12  FORMAT  ('+' ,T10, ' _____ ' ,T25, ' _____ ')
```

The first WRITE/FORMAT sends a column header to the printer where, because the first character of the line is a 1, it is printed at the top of the page. The second WRITE/FORMAT sends a line that will be printed without skipping; it underlines the first header.

A common error made by a beginning programmer is to forget about the first character rule. Assume, for example, that N = 123. What would be printed by the following statements:

```
WRITE  (6,22)  N

22  FORMAT  (I3)
```

The answer may surprise you. At the top of a page, the number 23 will be printed! Why? Because the 1 is treated as a carriage control character. It controls printer spacing, and is not printed. Remember to code a carriage control character as the first item in a FORMAT statement, or at least to skip the first position or two (X or tab), and you won't make this mistake.

Another common beginner's problem is not allowing enough space to hold a complete number. Assume, for example, that the value of the variable X is 5.25. You might be tempted to use F3.2 as your FORMAT item, but that would be wrong. Why? The first digit following the F does *not* signify the number of *digits* in the output field. It signifies the number of *positions* in the output field. The decimal point *will be* printed. It occupies a print position. F4.2 would be correct. *Be sure to allow space for the decimal point.*

A negative sign presents a similar problem. Assume, for example, that K = 12. The FORMAT item I2 would be correct for printing K. What happens, however, if the value of K is changed to –12? Now, I2 is wrong. The sign will be printed for a negative number, and the sign occupies one print position. If a value can be negative, *be sure to allow space for the sign.*

Sometimes, the programmer will simply make a mistake and not allow enough room in the FORMAT item. Perhaps a program logic error will generate a larger than anticipated answer. If a FORMAT item is not sufficient to hold the value of its matching variable, most versions of FORTRAN will print an error flag, such as:

```
*******
```

Whenever you see a string of asterisks in your output, you can assume that you have an invalid FORMAT item. Having isolated the problem, you should be able to figure out what went wrong.

Another common beginner's error is best described by looking at an example:

FIELD = 75.52

WRITE (6,35) FEILD

35 FORMAT (5X,F5.2)

Do you see what happened? We assigned a value to FIELD, and then tried to print the value of FEILD, spelling the variable name incorrectly. You will probably do it at least once before the term ends.

What would the computer do? Under some versions of FORTRAN, an attempt will be made to print whatever is in FEILD. Other versions are more helpful, and the programmer will find:

UUUUU

printed in the output field. A string of U's indicates that the variable listed in a WRITE statement was undefined; in other words, the program had not assigned a value to the variable. If you encounter this problem, look carefully for variations in the spelling of a variable name.

A FINAL COMMENT

FORMAT statements are not difficult to use. Yes, they are tedious, and they must be precise, but the problems are largely mechanical, and not logical. Skill in using FORMAT statements is achieved through practice, period. After you have written a few programs that use FORMAT statements, the mild confusion you may now be experiencing should disappear.

EXERCISES

1. Write a reasonable FORMAT item for each of the following numbers:

     a. your age.

     b. your grade point average.

     c. the frequency of your favorite radio station.

     d. the speed, in revolutions per minute, of a stereo
         turntable playing an album.

     e. the speed limit on a major highway.

2. Assume an input record contains the following fields:

Positions	Contents
1-8	an identification number
9-10	blank
11-14	an hourly pay rate correct to two decimal places
15-20	blank
21-23	hours worked correct to 1 decimal place
24-30	blank
31-33	department number

Code a FORMAT statement to read this record.

3. You are about to write a program to compute and print the square roots of the numbers from 1 to 100. Each square root is to be printed correct to four decimal places. Code FORMAT statements for a set of column headers *and* for the detail lines that will display each number and its square root.

4. Assume that a report in your bank contains the following information for each checking account customer: the customer number, the start-of-day account balance, the sum of all checks cashed today, the sum of all deposits received today, and the end-of-day account balance. Write FORMAT statements for a header and for a data line. Don't forget to place the header at the top of a page. Assume an 8-digit customer number. Assume a maximum of one million for each dollar field. Remember that the end-of-day balance can be negative.

4

Branching
and Looping:
More Complex Loops

OVERVIEW

In Chapter 3, we planned and coded two programs using a simple counter as the loop control. The programs to be developed in this chapter will require more complex loop structures. The first program will compare the changing populations of two countries. The main loop will be executed repetitively until a critical condition, computed within the loop, is reached. The second program will create a table of wind chill factors using loops similar to the count loops of Chapter 3. The formula for computing a wind chill factor, however, involves two variables: temperature and wind velocity. To control two variables we will need two loops, one inside the other—nested loops.

No new FORTRAN instructions will be needed for the population program. The concept of predefined functions will be introduced with the second program.

A CRITICAL CONDITION LOOP: POPULATION STATISTICS

In mid-1979, the population of the United States was estimated at 226 million, while Mexico's was estimated at 66 million. The United States had, however, almost reached zero population growth, with an annual growth rate of only 0.9%, while Mexico's population was increasing at a 2.8% rate. Clearly, if the 1979 growth rates were to continue, there might come a time when the population of Mexico would surpass the United States'. Given the growth rates described above, when would this condition be expected to occur?

Developing the algorithms is the key to this problem. What do we mean by growth rate? How does the growth rate affect the population? The growth rate is simply a measure of the amount by which a population increases each year. In any given year, some people are born and some die; some people immigrate, and others emigrate. If the number of people added to a population is greater than the number who leave, the growth rate is positive; otherwise it's negative. A growth rate of 2.8% means that Mexico's population increased by this amount during 1979.

Let's use a simple example to develop our algorithms. We'll imagine that a tiny country called Nowhere has a population of 1000 people, with a growth rate of 10%. During the first year of our study, the population will increase by 10% of that 1000 people; in other words, the population *increase* will be 100 people. What will the population of Nowhere be at the end of the year? If we had 1000 at the start, and added a net total of 100, there will be 1100 people at the end of the year. What happens during the second year? We have 1100 as the year starts. The population increases by 10%—110 new people are added. The population at year's end will be 1210. Those 100 people who joined the population during year 1 will have children of their own, or be joined by friends or relatives immigrating from other countries; they contribute to growth, too.

Now, let's generalize. Let X be the population of the country as the year begins. Let "i" be the growth rate. The increase in population for the year will be:

$$\text{net increase} = Xi,$$

or the product of the population and the growth rate. What will the population be at the end of the year? The sum of the start of year population, X, and the population growth, Xi. Expressed algebraically:

$$\text{end-of-year population} = X + Xi$$

If you are familiar with algebra, you know that we can factor this relationship to get:

$$\text{end-of-year population} = X(1+i)$$

What is the population at the beginning of year two? The same as the population at the end of year one; in other words:

$$X_2 = X(1+i)$$

If this relationship were placed in a loop and executed repetitively, it could start with the population at time zero, compute the population at the end of the first year, then use this new population to find the number of people at the end of the second year, and so on.

The growth rate for the United States (in 1979) was 0.9%. If we let the variable USPOP stand for the population of the U.S., then the statement:

USPOP = USPOP * (1.0 + 0.009)

or:

USPOP = USPOP * 1.009

can be used to compute the expected population of the country in each of a series of years. Likewise, if the growth rate for Mexico were 2.8%, and MEXPOP represents the population, the statement:

MEXPOP = MEXPOP * 1.028

can be used to compute the year-by-year population of Mexico. We have our algorithms.

Beyond defining the algorithms, the logic of the program is really quite simple (Fig. 4.1). The populations of the two countries are initialized, and the year is set to (in this example) 1979. Then we enter our loop. The 1980 populations of both Mexico and the United States are computed and compared. If Mexico still has fewer people than the United States, the program returns to the top of the loop, where populations for 1981 are computed and compared. The loop continues until the condition "population of Mexico is less than population of U.S." is no longer true. All that remains is to print the two populations and the year when Mexico moves ahead.

Writing the program should be easy; a version is shown as Fig. 4.2. Note the REAL statement at the beginning of the program; why must MEXPOP be defined as real? Note that there is no input to this program. The result (2045) is shown at the end of Fig. 4.2.

NESTED LOOPS: PREPARING A WIND CHILL FACTOR TABLE

If you live in an area where the winter temperature sometimes drops below thirty degrees, you have probably heard of the wind chill factor. The idea is really quite simple. As anyone who has been out in the cold knows, the degree of discomfort or the risk of frostbite are not only functions of temperature. On a windless day, twenty degrees may be quite comfortable, but when a brisk wind is blowing, that same twenty degrees seems intolerable. Just as the summertime combination of heat and humidity is worse than the heat alone, the wintertime combination of cold and wind is far worse than just the cold. In fact, this latter combination can be deadly.

The wind chill factor is a number used to measure the combined effect of low temperature and wind. By plugging the temperature (in Fahrenheit) and the wind

Fig. 4.1: *The logic of the population problem.*

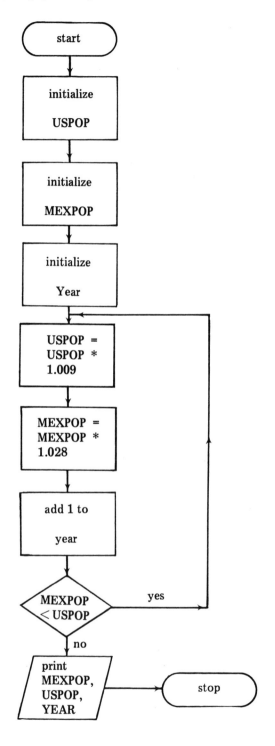

Fig. 4.2: *The population program.*

```
C                                        *  PROGRAM TO DETERMINE WHEN POPULATION
C                                        *  OF UNITED STATES AND POPULATION OF
C                                        *  MEXICO ARE EQUAL.
C                                        *     INITIAL CONDITIONS:
C                                        *        POP U.S.         226 MILLION
C                                        *        POP MEXICO        66 MILLION
C                                        *        GROWTH, US        0.9%
C                                        *        GROWTH, MEX       2.8%
C                                        *        YEAR             1979
C                                        *  WRITTEN BY: W.S. DAVIS
C                                        *              1/10/81
C                                        *  * * * * * * * * * * * * * * * * * *
      REAL MEXPOP
      INTEGER YEAR
      USPOP = 226000000.
      MEXPOP = 66000000.
      YEAR = 1979
   10 USPOP = USPOP * 1.009
      MEXPOP = MEXPOP * 1.028
      YEAR = YEAR + 1
      IF (MEXPOP .LT. USPOP) GO TO 10
      WRITE (6,11) USPOP,MEXPOP,YEAR
      STOP
   11 FORMAT (5X,'POP US = ',F11.0,5X,'POP MEX = ',F11.0,5X,'IN ',I4)
      END

$ENTRY
 POP US =    408237800.     POP MEX =    408395700.      IN 2045
```

velocity (in miles per hour) into a formula, an "equivalent temperature" is computed; in theory, this temperature (with no wind) is equivalent to the given combination of temperature and wind. For example, a day on which the temperature is 20 degrees and the wind is blowing 20 miles per hour will seem as cold as a day when the temperature is minus five degrees and there is no wind.

You may be able to find the formula for computing a wind chill factor in a basic science textbook, a text on meteorology, or an encyclopedia. However, it is not generally available; thus, rather than asking you to find it, we'll list it below:

$$\text{WCF} = 91.4 - (.288\sqrt{\text{WIND}} + .450 - .019 \ \text{WIND}) \quad (91.4 - \text{TEMP}),$$

where "WIND" is the wind velocity in miles per hour and "TEMP" is measured in degrees Fahrenheit.

How do you react when faced with such a formula? Many people simply panic when they see all those terms. Don't. Break the formula into pieces; it's much easier to handle that way. We might, for example, use the following steps:

$$\text{WCF1} = (.288\sqrt{\text{WIND}} + .450 - .019 \ \text{WIND})$$

$$\text{WCF2} = (91.4 - \text{TEMP})$$

$$\text{WCF} = 91.4 - (\text{WCF1} * \text{WCF2})$$

(Using these three simple steps will also decrease the risk of typing errors as we begin to code our FORTRAN program.)

Now that we have the algorithm, let's consider how we might structure a program to generate a table of wind chill factors. We would like to pick a temperature, 20 degrees Fahrenheit, for example, and then compute the wind chill factors associated with this temperature in combination with a variety of wind velocities. We might describe this logic as:

1. initialize temperature,

2. initialize wind velocity,

    3. compute wind chill factor,

    4. print temperature, wind velocity, and wind chill factor,

    5. increment to next wind velocity,

    6. if wind velocity is less than or equal to the desired upper limit, go back to step number 3.

It's a simple loop, similar in many ways to the count loops of Chapter 3.

What next? Once a series of wind chill factors has been computed for a given temperature, we might want to select another temperature and repeat the loop. Assume, for example, that we want wind chill factors for wind velocities ranging from 10 to 50 miles per hour, and for temperatures from -30 up to 30 degrees Fahrenheit. Of course, we could obtain the desired output by executing the logic described above, then changing the instruction that initializes the temperature and rerunning the program. It would be easier, however, to include the instructions needed to change the value of temperature in the program. Consider, for example, the following logic:

1. initialize temperature,

    2. initialize wind velocity,

    3. compute wind chill factor,

    4. print temperature, wind velocity, and wind chill factor,

    5. increment to next wind velocity,

    6. if wind velocity is less than or equal to the desired upper limit, go back to step number 3.

7. increment to next temperature,

8. if temperature is less than or equal to desired upper limit, go back to step number 2.

These steps are shown graphically in Fig. 4.3.

Steps 2 through 6 have intentionally been indented to better show their relationship to steps 1, 7, and 8. We have a loop within a loop. The **outer loop** controls the value of temperature. The **inner loop**, which is part of the outer loop, controls the value of the wind velocity. The first time through the outer loop, temperature will be initialized, and then the inner loop will be repeated many times. After the inner loop has been processed the specified number of times, a second cycle of the outer loop begins; once again the inner loop will be repeated several times. The two loops are said to be **nested**.

When two or more loops are nested, one loop is coded *completely* inside another (Fig. 4.4). It is legal to have one loop within another loop, within yet another loop, and so on—multiple levels of nesting. Some versions of FORTRAN may limit the number of levels of nesting, but on most the only real limit is the programmer's ability to keep track of what is going on. Two "nested" loops may *not* overlap (Fig. 4.4 again).

In general, the structure of the wind chill factor program is shown in Fig. 4.5. Note that two DO loops are nested, one to control the temperature, and the other to control the wind velocity. A few new FORTRAN features must be introduced before the formula can be coded, however.

One term in the wind chill factor formula calls for the square root of the wind velocity. What exactly is a square root? The square root of X is a number which, when multiplied by itself, gives X. How is a square root computed? Unfortunately, there is no easy way to compute a square root directly; normally, square roots are estimated. How can a FORTRAN programmer obtain a reasonable estimate of the square root of a number?

Square roots can be estimated in two ways. First, a square root is simply the ½ power of a number; in other words:

X**0.5

means the same thing as $\sqrt{X}$. Writing X**0.5 will produce an estimate of the square root of X. This technique can be used to find any root of a number. For example, the cube root of X is

X**(1/3)

and the fourth root is:

X**0.25   or   X**(1/4).

Square roots are much more common in mathematical analysis than cube roots or fourth roots. Thus a special FORTRAN predefined function has been developed to provide an accurate estimate of a square root. By coding:

SQRT(X)

Fig. 4.3: *The logic of the wind chill factor program.*

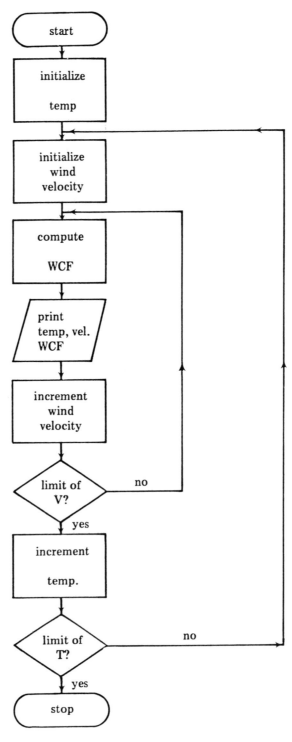

Fig. 4.4: *Nested Loop structures.*

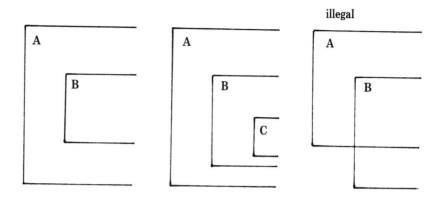

Fig. 4.5: *The structure of the wind chill factor program.*

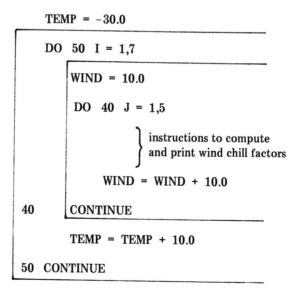

in an expression, the programmer can take advantage of this predefined function, which is available on most versions of FORTRAN.

Usually, other functions are available as well. They provide estimates of common trigonometric functions, exponential values, logarithms, absolute values, random numbers, and other commonly used mathematical terms; a list of FORTRAN functions is provided in Module C, immediately following this chapter.

Now, we can write the assignments statements for computing a wind chill factor. Using TEMP for the temperature, WIND for the wind velocity, and WCF for the wind chill factor, the following three statements will perform the desired computations:

WCF1 = (0.288 * SQRT(WIND)) + 0.45 - (0.019 * WIND)

WCF2 = 91.4 - TEMP

WCF = 91.4 - (WCF1 * WCF2)

Generally, wind chill factors are shown as whole numbers. The computed factor for 0 degrees Fahrenheit and a wind velocity of 20 miles per hour is -32.7189 degrees; this would be shown as -32 degrees. How can we convert the fractional numbers generated within the computer to whole number (or integer) form? We can simply, in an explicit type statement, define WCF as an integer variable. When the third assignment statement is executed, the result of a series of real computations will be converted to integer form.

A completed version of the wind chill program is shown as Fig. 4.6. You should have little trouble following the logic. Note that a set of column headers is printed *before* the nested loops begin. Why is the statement to WRITE headers placed here? Note also that the statements comprising the inner loop are clearly indented; in effect, indentation visually defines the loop structure. The output generated by this program is shown as Fig. 4.7.

Note that the values of TEMP and WIND are initialized and incremented in assignment statements; why didn't we simply use these variables as DO loop control variables? All computations are real; thus TEMP and WIND should be real. A real variable cannot be used as a DO loop control. Also, on most versions of FORTRAN, it is illegal to initialize a DO loop control variable with a negative value. The first value of TEMP is to be -30.0.

How would you test the wind chill factor program? Select a few sets of values from the table and do the calculations with a pocket calculator. You should be able to generate approximately the same answers. If not, first check your own computations, then check your algorithms.

SUMMARY

In this chapter, we wrote two programs involving somewhat more-complex loop structures. The first was a population program. The populations and growth rates of

```
      INTEGER WCF
      WRITE (6,11)
      TEMP = -30.0
      DO 50 I=1.7
         WIND = 10.0
         DO 40 J=1.5
            WCF1 = (0.288 * SQRT(WIND)) + 0.450 - (0.019 * WIND)
            WCF2 = 91.4 - TEMP
            WCF = 91.4 - (WCF1 * WCF2)
            WRITE (6,12) TEMP,WIND,WCF
            WIND = WIND + 10.0
40       CONTINUE
         TEMP = TEMP + 10.0
50    CONTINUE
      STOP
11    FORMAT ('1',T10,'TEMP',T20,'WIND-MPH',T30,'WCF')
12    FORMAT (T10,F4.0,T20,F4.0,T30,I3)
      END
```

Fig. 4.6: *The wind chill factor program.*

TEMP	WIND-MPH	WCF
-30.	10.	-50
-30.	20.	-73
-30.	30.	-85
-30.	40.	-92
-30.	50.	-95
-20.	10.	-39
-20.	20.	-59
-20.	30.	-70
-20.	40.	-76
-20.	50.	-79
-10.	10.	-27
-10.	20.	-46
-10.	30.	-56
-10.	40.	-61
-10.	50.	-64
0.	10.	-15
0.	20.	-32
0.	30.	-41
0.	40.	-46
0.	50.	-49
10.	10.	-3
10.	20.	-19
10.	30.	-27
10.	40.	-31
10.	50.	-33
20.	10.	7
20.	20.	-5
20.	30.	-12
20.	40.	-16
20.	50.	-18
30.	10.	19
30.	20.	8
30.	30.	1
30.	40.	-1
30.	50.	-2

Fig. 4.7: *The output from the wind chill factor program.*

THIS PROGRAM PRINTS A WIND CHILL
FACTOR TABLE. GIVEN THE TEMPERATURE
AND THE WIND VELOCITY (IN MPH), THE
WIND CHILL FACTOR IS COMPUTED FROM
A FORMULA.
      TABLE ENTRIES WILL BE FOR WIND
VELOCITIES RANGING FROM 10 TO 50
MPH AND FOR TEMPERATURES RANGING
FROM -30 TO 30 DEGREES.
      WRITTEN BY: W.S. DAVIS
                  1/10/81

99

Mexico and the United States were given. The question was: When will Mexico's population overtake the United States'?

The program basically involved a loop. Within the loop the populations of the two countries were computed year by year, and then compared. As long as Mexico's population was less than that of the United States, the loop was repeated; as soon as this condition no longer held, the loop was terminated and the answer printed. The key idea was controlling a loop by using values generated within the loop. Actually, the most significant problem faced in this example was defining the algorithms.

The second problem involved nested loops. The program was designed to generate a table of wind chill factors. Once again, defining the algorithm was the first problem. Once the algorithm was defined, we turned to the structure of the program, describing it as a loop within a loop. The FORTRAN predefined function SQRT was introduced.

EXERCISES

1. Add to the chapter example that computed a table of wind chill factors, the logic needed to *round* to the nearest integer. Hints: add 0.5 before converting to integer. Look into the INT predefined function.

2. Given the populations and growth rates of the first example, estimate the combined populations of the United States and Mexico in the year 2000.

3. Once again using the populations and growth rates of the first example, in what year will the population of the United States be expected to pass 300 million?

4. Modify the wind chill factor program so that it generates a table for temperatures from −20 to 40 degrees, and wind velocities ranging from 5 to 50 MPH in increments of 5.

5. An individual borrows $1000 and agrees to pay it back in a series of $50 payments. Interest is charged at 1.5 percent per month on the unpaid balance. The first few payments might be summarized as follows:

Month	Beginning Balance	Total Payment	Interest	Principle	Ending Balance
1	1000.00	50.00	15.00	35.00	965.00
2	965.00	50.00	14.48	35.52	929.48
3	929.48	50.00	13.94	36.06	893.42

Note that the beginning balance for any given month is the same as the ending balance for the preceeding month. Note also that the interest is always 0.015 times the beginning balance, and the amount credited to interest is always $50.00 minus the amount of interest.

Write a program to list this table until the ending balance is zero.

6. Generalize problem number 6 to input the amount of the loan, the monthly payment, and the interest rate. Then generate a month-by-month table until the ending balance is zero.

7. One technique for estimating the square root of a number is based on Newton's method. The programmer provides an initial "guess" of the square root. This guess (x) is then plugged into the formula:

$$EST = 0.5 * (X + (T/X)),$$

where: EST is the new estimate,

X is the "first guess" or a prior estimate,

T is the number whose square root you wish to find,

yielding a new estimate of the square root. This new estimate is then substituted for X in the formula, and another new estimate is generated. This process continues until the answer is "close enough". How can the program tell when this condition is met? If the value of:

$$ABS \ [\frac{X - EST}{X}]$$

is less than a very small value selected by the programmer (0.0001 for example), the degree of error in the estimate is said to be close enough.

Write a program to input T, the number whose square root is to be found, and X, an initial estimate. Use Newton's method to estimate the square root.

8. Add to program number 7 the instructions needed to compute and print the square root of T as generated by T**0.5 and as generated by SQRT(T), along with your own estimate. Compare the results.

9. A technique for integration easily applied to the computer involves dividing the area under any curve into a series of rectangles, computing the area of each rectangle, and then summing the areas. Initially, the area might be divided into two rectangles, then four, eight, sixteen, and so on. With each cycle, the sum of the areas of the triangles will be closer and closer to the actual area under the curve. Write a program to integrate the area under a curve using this technique. Make up your own function, or use $Y = 1.5 \ X^2$, for values X between 1 and 10. Define an acceptable solution as one for which the "prior" estimate and the "new" estimate differ by less than 0.01%.

10. Using combinations of half-dollars, quarters, nickels, dimes, and pennies, how many different ways can one make change for a dollar?

11. Write a program to generate a multiplication table.

12. Write a program to make change. Read the amount of a purchase and the amount paid; the difference is the amount of change due the customer. (Be careful, it may be negative.) Print the total amount of change due and list the composition of this change: i.e., how many dollars, half-dollars, nickels, dimes, quarters, and pennies should be given to the customer?

13. Write a program to generate a sales tax table. Start with a purchase of 10 cents, and assume a tax of 1 cent on this amount. Given a tax rate of 5%, increment the amount of the purchase 1 cent at a time and compute the amount of tax due on this new amount. As soon as the computed amount of tax *exceeds* 1 cent, you have located the lower bound of the next tax bracket. Print 10 cents, the value one less than the critical point you have just discovered, and the amount of the tax—1 cent. Now, using the just computed critical point as a lower bound, find the point at which the computed tax exceeds 2 cents; this defines the lower bound of the next tax bracket. Print the lower and upper bounds and the tax amount. Continue until the amount of the sale reaches $10.00.

14. Earlier, you wrote a program to compute the value of the $24 the Indians were paid for Manhatten Island, had they invested their money; the formula is:

$$P = 24 (1 + i)^n,$$

where i is the interest rate and "n" is the number of years. Use 8.5% interest; the property was sold in 1626. Show the value of the money at 50 year intervals.

15. The mathematical constant e is the limit of $(1 + 1/n)^n$ as n approaches infinity. Write a program to estimate a value for e. Stop when the difference between two successive estimates is less than 0.0001. Print the values of e and n.

16. The sine of a number is defined by the formula:

$$\sin x = x - (x^3/3!) + (x^5/5!) - (x^7/7!) \ldots$$

where 3! is the factorial of 3. Write a program to read a value of x and estimate the sin. An acceptable answer is defined as one for which the error is less than 0.01%. Compare your answer with the one generated by the predefined function SIN(X).

17. "It's not the heat, it's the humidity." This common summer-time complaint recognizes that the discomfort an individual feels is due to the humidity as well as the heat. In fact, there is a measure of this degree of discomfort analogous to the wind chill factor. The temperature/humidity index is computed from the formula:

$$THI = TEMP - (0.55 - 0.55RH) \ (TEMP - 58),$$

where TEMP is in degrees Fahrenheit, and RH is the relative humidity in decimal form (60% is .60).

Write a program to create a table of temperature/humidity indexes for temperatures ranging from 70 degrees to 110 degrees and for relative humidities, ranging from 60% to 100%. Use increments of 5 in both cases.

Module C

FORTRAN
Predefined Functions

OVERVIEW

Certain mathematical terms are encountered with such frequency that special pre-defined functions have been developed to compute or estimate them. This module describes the functions that are commonly available in FORTRAN.

105

AN EXAMPLE

Assume that a FORTRAN program is to compute value of the following algebraic equation:

$$C = \sqrt{a^2 + b^2}$$

Some of you may recognize this as the formula for computing the length of the third side of a triangle, given the other two. An assignment statement to perform these computations would be:

$$C = SQRT(A**2 + B**2)$$

SQRT is a *predefined function*. The expression enclosed in parentheses is called the *argument*. Essentially what happens is that the value of the argument is computed (do what is enclosed within the parentheses first). Then the value of the argument is passed to the square root function, and the root is estimated. The result in effect replaces the reference to the SQRT function. Finally, in this example, the estimated square root will be stored at variable C.

All the predefined functions are used in much the same way; simply code the function name followed by an argument enclosed in a set of parentheses. The argument can be a constant, a variable, or an expression. It can even contain a reference to another function. You can use predefined functions in much the same way that you use constants or variables in building an expression.

Note that you cannot code:

$$150 \quad LET \quad SQRT(X) = 25.0$$

The built-in function is *not* a variable, so it cannot be coded to the left of the equal sign.

A TABLE OF COMMON PREDEFINED FUNCTIONS

The following predefined functions are available in FORTRAN 77. In each case, X is used to represent the argument, which may be a constant, a variable, or an expression. Not all functions are listed.

Function	Returns
ABS(X)	The absolute value of the argument.
COS(X)	The cosine of the argument. The argument must be expressed in radians, and must be real.
EXP(X)	The value of e^X. The argument must be real.

INT(X)	The greatest integer which is less than or equal to the argument. Often used to convert a real argument to integer form.
LOG(X)	The natural logarithm of the argument. The argument must be real.
LOG10(X)	Common (base 10) logarithm of the argument. The argument must be real.
MAX(X1,X2, . . .)	Largest of the arguments.
MIN(X1,X2, . . .)	Smallest of the arguments.
REAL(I)	Value of the argument in real form. Often used to convert an integer argument to real form.
SIN(X)	The sin of the argument. The argument must be expressed in radians. The argument must be real.
SQRT(X)	The square root of the argument. Note that the argument may not be negative. The argument must be real.
TAN(X)	The tangent of the argument. The argument must be expressed in radians. The argument must be real.

5

Structure and Style: Modular Program Design

OVERVIEW

Thus far, the programs we have considered have been relatively simple: most "real world" programs are much more complex. In this chapter we will investigate techniques for dealing with such problems. When faced with a complex programming assignment, the good programmer will often subdivide it into a series of simple modules, attacking each as an independent problem. When these simple modules are combined, a program to solve the more complex problem can be constructed. This modular approach to program design is perhaps the most important single concept that the beginning programmer can learn.

FORTRAN subroutines will be introduced to support the ideas of this chapter.

PROGRAM COMPLEXITY

Real world problems are frequently quite complex; computer programs tend to reflect this complexity. Consider, for example, the common business data processing problem of computing a payroll. On the surface, the structure of this problem is simple. To compute payroll for any given individual:

1. compute gross pay (generally, the product of hours worked and an hourly pay rate),

2. compute the amount of each deduction, including federal income tax, state income tax, local income tax, social security tax, and others,

3. subtract the deductions from gross pay to get net (takehome) pay.

Where is the complexity? It lies beneath the surface, within the individual, detailed computations.

Gross pay provides a good example. Most of us tend to think of gross pay as a simple computation: if you work for 30 hours, and your pay rate is $5.00 per hour, your gross pay is the product of these two numbers, $150.00. There is much more to it, however. What about overtime? Typically, hours over 40 in any given week are paid at 1½ times the regular rate. What about shift premium? Often, people who work on the night shift receive an extra 8 to 10 percent. How can we handle bonus payments? What about the salesperson who is paid a commission? Managers and other professionals are often paid a salary rather than an hourly wage; how is their pay computed?

These are but a few of the questions that must be answered before the payroll program can be coded. Each of the taxes, and each of the other deductions can be equally complex. The broad structure of the program *is* simple; it is easy to see, in general, what must be done. The detailed computations are complex. Combining a large gross pay routine, a large income tax routine, and several other large computational routines produces a very large (and hence very complex) program. How do professional programmers deal with this complexity?

MODULAR PROGRAMMING: DIVIDE AND CONQUER

The solution is to divide the program into pieces, and then to attack the pieces one at a time. It is relatively easy to write the instructions to compute gross pay, even with all the complicated rules. It is relatively easy to write a program to compute federal income tax. The problem is one of dealing with *all* this complexity at one time. Don't! Solve a series of little problems one at a time; then put the pieces together. This is the essence of modular programming.

Modular program design provides a framework for planning a complex program. We begin by defining, broadly, the function to be performed: in our payroll example, that function is to compute payroll. Now, we can begin to define the specific tasks needed to complete this primary function. In general, to compute payroll we must:

1. read a set of payroll data,

2. compute gross pay,

3. compute social security tax,

4. compute income tax,

5. compute other deductions (we won't list them all),

6. compute net pay,

7. print a paycheck.

These steps will be repeated for each employee. A graphic view of the program as we now see it is shown in Fig. 5.1. This is called a **hierarchy chart**; it shows the relationship between the modules that compose the program.

The module at the top of Fig. 5.1 is called the **mainline** or control module. Its function is to tie together all the second-level routines, controlling the order in which they are executed. The mainline will begin by telling the first of the level-II modules to "read a record". The actual instructions to accomplish the input operation will be found in this second level module. When the task is completed, control is returned to the mainline, which tells the second of the level-II modules to "compute gross pay". Once again, the detailed computations are carried out by this lower-level module; once again control is returned to the mainline. Each secondary routine or **subroutine** is executed in turn, but always under control of the mainline.

What is the advantage of structuring a program this way? Very simply, each subroutine can be written independently. As a result, we can write the code needed to compute gross pay, and then write the code needed to compute income tax without worrying about how the gross pay module was written. If the program becomes too lengthy, we can subdivide responsiblity, assigning the subroutines to different programmers. As we shall see, this structure greatly simplifies writing and developing a complex program.

After the program is complete, other advantages accrue. Consider, for example, the problem of locating and fixing a bug. Assume that income tax is being incorrectly computed. Since all the code for computing income tax is contained in a single module, the programmer can ignore the bulk of the program and concentrate on this relatively small routine. Almost immediately the search is narrowed; as a result the bug is easier to find and to correct. This simplification in program "debugging" is a consequence of the structure of the program.

Program maintenance is also greatly simplified. What happens when the federal government passes new laws that change income tax withholding rates? Since all tax computations are found in a single subroutine, the most we will have to do is rewrite that subroutine; the rest of the program can be left as is. What happens when a new

111

union contract changes the rules for computing gross pay? Once again, only one subroutine is affected. To the student who (typically) writes a program and then discards it at the end of the semester, this ease of maintenance may not seem significant. However, maintenance is a critical concern to the professional programmer who must debug someone else's (bad) code.

Philosophically, modular programming seems to make sense. Let's get more concrete. How can we go about designing and developing a program in modular style? Where do we start?

The mainline is the key to the program: it ties the entire program together. Thus the obvious place to start is with the mainline. Of course, we are not ready to deal with all the details, so we won't. Instead, we will write a skeleton mainline, with all functions securely in place, but at a very superficial level.

The Skeleton Mainline

What is a skeleton mainline? Essentially, it's an outline. Like an outline, a skeleton mainline shows the specific steps that will be included in the finished product, and clearly defines the sequence of these steps. The only thing missing is the detail.

Earlier in the chapter, we described the functions that must be performed to compute an individual's pay, including:

1. read a set of payroll data,

2. compute gross pay,

3. compute social security tax,

4. compute income tax,

5. compute net pay,

6. print a paycheck.

In a typical payroll program, other deductions will be involved, but this outline is sufficient for our purposes.

Given this outline, our next task is to define a simple (but realistic) algorithm for implementing each function. Gross pay, for example, is defined as the product of hours worked and an hourly pay rate. Social security tax is simply 6.65 percent of gross pay. Ten percent of gross might represent a reasonable estimate of income tax. Finally, net pay is gross pay minus both social security tax and income tax. Of course these algorithms are not entirely correct. There are merely *dummy* algorithms designed to allow us to write a skeleton mainline.

What about output data? Clearly, if we are to write a paycheck, we must have the employee's name and a computed amount for net pay. We know where net pay comes from—the algorithm we just defined. Where does the name come from? It must come from the first input operation. What other values will be needed on input? Hours

Fig. 5.1: *A hierarchy chart of the payroll program.*

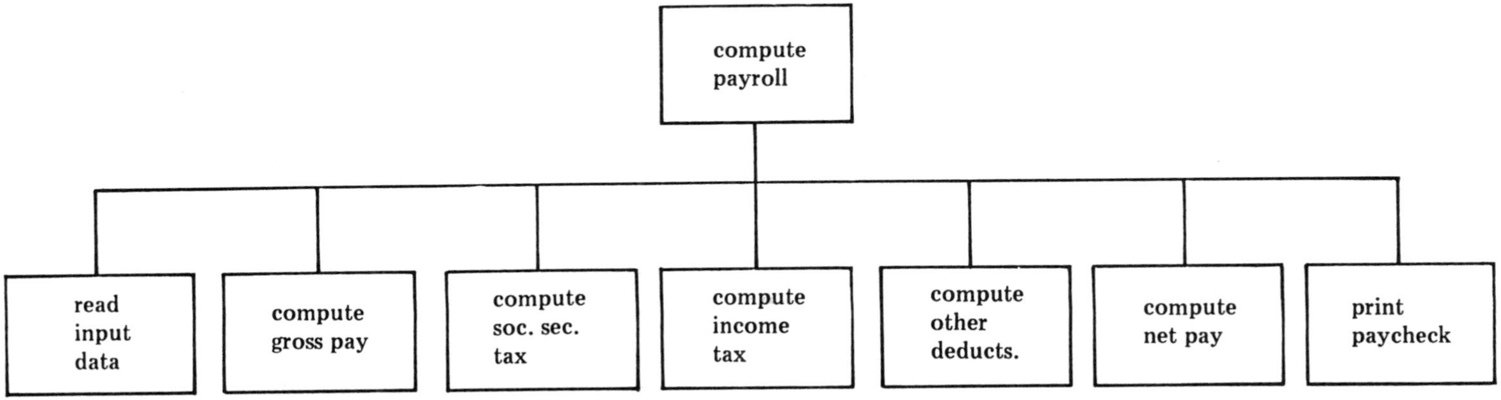

worked and the hourly pay rate must be available before gross pay can be computed, so they must come from the input record.

A simple flowchart of the skeleton mainline can now be prepared (Fig. 5.2). A program to implement this logic is shown as Fig. 5.3.

The program of Fig. 5.3 contains two new FORTRAN features. First, two of the values that are read into the program—the employee's name and initials—are *character* rather than numeric values. Character variables are defined by simply listing them in a CHARACTER statement at the beginning of the program. Character variables may not be used in arithmetic expressions. It is possible to assign a value to a character variable; for example:

NAME = 'SMITH'

or:

NAME1 = NAME2

A character variable can be compared to another character variable or to a literal constant in an IF statement; for example:

IF (NAME .EQ. 'JONES') THEN DO

How long is a character field? A last name might call for ten or fifteen characters. A person's initials require only two. An address might occupy twenty or more. The point is that a character field can be almost any length. Normally, the programmer will specify the length of a field in the CHARACTER statement. For example, variables listed after CHARACTER*2 (Fig. 5.3) will hold two characters, while those listed after CHARACTER*16 will hold sixteen.

The other new FORTRAN feature in Fig. 5.3 concerns the test for end of data. Previously, we defined a sentinel value (such as a negative number), placed this value at the end of the deck or entered it after the last "real" input record, and tested for this condition following the READ.

Think back to Chapter 2, where a deck of cards (or card images) was prepared for submission to the FORTRAN compiler (Fig. 2.4). Remember the control cards? The last card in the deck, a $EOJ card in our example, clearly marked the end of the data. Why not test for the $EOJ card? That is exactly what we are going to do in the payroll program. Look carefully at the READ statement. An extra field has been added inside the parentheses:

10 READ (5,11,END=99) NAME,INIT,HOURS,RATE

The "END=" option tells the computer where to branch when the end-of-data record is encountered; in effect, this option says, "If the first four positions on the card are $EOJ, GO TO 99". Other systems use different characters to designate the end of data condition, but the idea is the same.

114

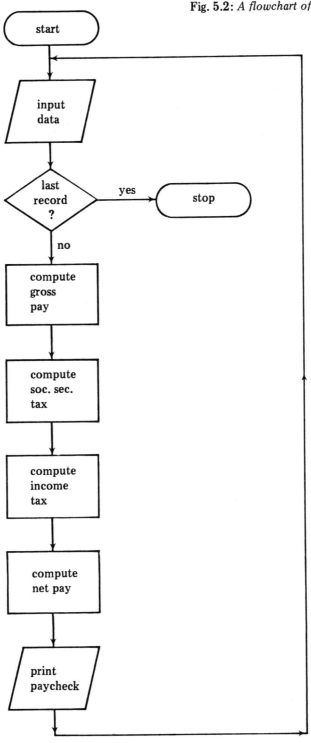

start

input
data

last
record
?

yes

stop

no

compute
gross
pay

compute
soc. sec.
tax

compute
income
tax

compute
net pay

print
paycheck

Fig. 5.3: *The skeleton mainline in FORTRAN.*

```
C     * THIS PROGRAM COMPUTES AND PRINTS
C     * AN INDIVIDUAL'S TAKE-HOME PAY.
C     *     WRITTEN BY: W.S. DAVIS
C     *                  1/10/81
C     * * * * * * * * * * * *

      REAL INCTAX,NETPAY
      CHARACTER*16 NAME
      CHARACTER*2 INIT

C     * THE PROGRAM STARTS BY READING
C     * AN INPUT RECORD CONTAINING AN
C     * EMPLOYEE'S NAME, INITIALS,
C     * HOURS WORKED, AND PAY RATE.

   10 READ (5,11,END=99) NAME,INIT,HOURS,RATE

C     * COMPUTE GROSS PAY AND
C     * SOCIAL SECURITY TAX.

      GROSS = HOURS * RATE
      SSTAX = GROSS * 0.0665

C     * COMPUTE INCOME TAX.

      INCTAX = GROSS * 0.10

C     * COMPUTE NET PAY AND PRINT CHECK;
C     * THEN GO BACK AND READ NEXT RECORD.

      NETPAY = GROSS - (SSTAX + INCTAX)
      WRITE (6,12) NAME,INIT,NETPAY
      GO TO 10

C     * * * * * * * * * * * * * * *
C     * AT END OF DATA, TERMINATE PROGRAM.*
C     * * * * * * * * * * * * * * *

   99 STOP
   11 FORMAT (A16,A2,F3.1,F4.2)
   12 FORMAT (5X,A16,' ',A2,3X,'$',F7.2)
      END
```

The First Subroutine: Gross Pay

What does the skeleton mainline tell us? Of what use is it? It defines the order in which computations are to be performed, a critical function in any program. We can test it; by running the skeleton mainline and inputting test data, we can verify that the program does, in fact, produce correct answers. It is time to begin adding functions.

Let's consider the gross pay computation first. How do we compute gross pay? Basically, it is the product of hours worked and an hourly pay rate. There is, however, more to it. We would like to add an overtime pay computation: all hours over 40 are paid at "time and a half".

Logically, what must we do to incorporate this new computation? The first step is to determine if overtime is to be paid. This involves a test: is "hours worked" greater than 40? If it is, gross pay will include overtime; if not, gross pay will be computed using the old rule (Fig. 5.4). We know the regular pay algorithm; using the variable names of the program, it is:

$$\text{GROSS} = \text{HOURS} * \text{RATE}$$

Fig. 5.4: *Gross pay logic.*

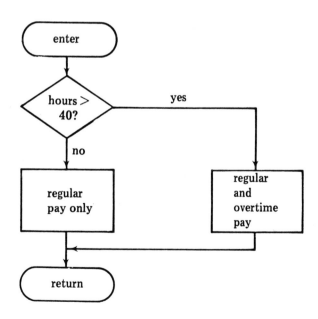

117

How do we compute overtime? Two computations will be involved. First, regular pay for the first 40 hours can be computed from:

$$GROSS = 40.0 * RATE$$

The number of hours of overtime is equal to the actual number of hours worked minus 40. These hours are paid at 1½ times the usual rate. Adding this algorithm to the earlier one yields:

$$GROSS = (40.0 * RATE) + (HOURS - 40.0) * (RATE * 1.5)$$

Do we really need all those parentheses? No, but they make the algorithm easier to read.

Subroutines

Now that we have the algorithms for computing gross pay, how can we add them to the skeleton mainline? One option, of course, is to simply incorporate the code, replacing the dummy assignment statement in the skeleton program with a series of assignment statements. The major problem with this approach is that gross pay logic is not the only module that must be added. We will eventually have to include detailed computations for income tax, social security tax, and numerous other deductions. If we simply incorporate all the instructions for computing all the deductions directly into the mainline, the program will become very lengthy, and *very* difficult to follow. Such programs are difficult to debug and difficult to maintain. There must be a better alternative.

There is. We can add the new code to the skeleton mainline by writing it in the form of a subroutine. What is a subroutine? Basically, a subroutine is an independent block of logic that performs a single, well-defined function. Consider, for example, the block diagram of Fig. 5.5. The function to be performed is COMPUTE GROSS PAY. If we provide values for HOURS and RATE to the subroutine, it will return a value for GROSS.

Fig. 5.5: *A block diagram of a subroutine.*

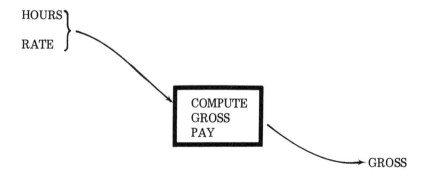

How does the FORTRAN programmer define a subroutine? First, it is necessary to clearly indicate that a given block of logic is, in fact, a subroutine. This is done by coding a **SUBROUTINE** statement:

SUBROUTINE module-name (variable-1,variable-2, . . .)

The "module-name" is simply the name of the subroutine; the rules for defining a subroutine name are the same as the rules for defining a FORTRAN variable. Following the subroutine name, enclosed in parentheses, is a list of variable names. Given certain values, a subroutine will perform computations and generate other values. The programmer must list all the variables that are to be passed to the subroutine, *and* all the variables returned by the subroutine.

For example, we are about to code a subroutine to compute gross pay. Values of HOURS and RATE must be provided to the subroutine; it will compute and return a value for GROSS. The following statement:

SUBROUTINE GROSUB (HOURS,RATE,GROSS)

might be used to define the subroutine.

Once the start of the subroutine has been defined, we can code the logic. A complete version of the gross pay routine for our developing program is shown in Fig. 5.6. Note how the variables listed in the SUBROUTINE statement are used in the computations. Note that the logic will always compute a value for GROSS. Finally,

Fig. 5.6: *The gross pay subroutine.*

```
      SUBROUTINE GROSUB (HOURS,RATE,GROSS)
C                             * * * * * * * * * * * * * * * *
C                             * SUBROUTINE TO COMPUTE GROSS PAY.
C                             * BASE PAY IS THE PRODUCT OF HOURS
C                             * WORKED AND THE HOURLY PAY RATE.
C                             * ALL HOURS WORKED OVER 40 ARE PAID
C                             * AT 1.5 TIMES THE REGULAR HOURLY
C                             * RATE.
C                             * * * * * * * * * * * * * * * *
      IF (HOURS .LE. 40.0) THEN DO
         GROSS = HOURS * RATE
      ELSE DO
         GROSS = 40.0*RATE + (HOURS-40.0)*(RATE*1.5)
      END IF
      RETURN
      END
```

note the last two statements in the routine: **RETURN** and **END**. You already know what the END statement does; it must be the last statement in a program. Since a subroutine is an independent module of FORTRAN code, it follows that it too should be terminated with an END statement. But what is the purpose of the RETURN statement? Let's investigate.

Linking the Subroutine to the Mainline

A subroutine, by itself, is rather useless. Our gross pay routine, for example, was designed to compute GROSS *given* HOURS and RATE. Where did HOURS and RATE come from? These two values *must have* come from the mainline. How is the computer to know that it is time to enter the subroutine and compute gross pay? The answer may seem a bit less obvious, but think about it. Some other program (that mainline again) must provide control. Let's put it another way. A subroutine is *part of* a larger program. The larger program must provide the subroutine's values, transfer control to the subroutine, and accept the subroutine's results.

How is this link between the mainline and the subroutine achieved? The key is another FORTRAN instruction—CALL:

> CALL module-name (variable-1,variable-2, . . .)

The key word CALL is followed by a subroutine name, which in turn is followed by a list of variables. For example, to CALL the gross pay subroutine, the programmer would code:

> CALL GROSUB (HOURS,RATE,GROSS)

The result would transfer control to the subroutine. Where should the CALL statement be placed? In our example, it would replace the simple computation of gross pay in the skeleton mainline.

Once control has been transferred to the subroutine, what happens? Basically, the instructions in the subroutine are executed. What happens when the subroutine instructions are finished? We want to go back to the main program and continue processing. That's the point of the RETURN instruction. It sends control back to the calling program.

Consider the logical flow sketched in Fig. 5.7. The mainline is in control as we begin. At some point, a CALL instruction is executed. Control is given to the subroutine, and its instructions are executed. Eventually, the RETURN instruction is encountered, and control goes back to the mainline instruction immediately following the CALL.

A version of the payroll program with the gross pay subroutine in place is shown in Fig. 5.8.

120

Fig. 5.7: *The CALL and RETURN statements.*

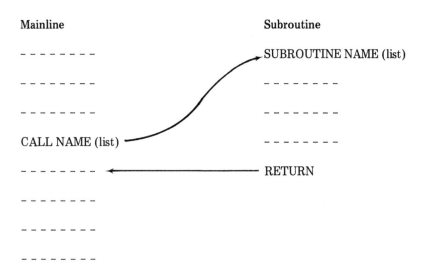

Passing Parameters

One potentially confusing factor in designing and using subroutines is the list of variables that follows the routine name in both the call statement and the SUBROUTINE statement. What does the variable list mean? How is it coded? A subroutine is an independent module. Normally, it contains no input or output statements. It's objective is to accept certain values from the mainline, perform a series of computations, and return the results to the mainline. The list, very simply, consists of the names of all variables that the mainline must pass to the subroutine *and* all variables that the subroutine must return. In the gross pay example, the mainline provided values of hours worked and an hourly pay rate, and the subroutine computed and returned the value of gross pay; thus the list contained HOURS, RATE, and GROSS.

Must the names listed in the CALL statement and the SUBROUTINE statement be the same? No. A subroutine is an independent module. Consider, for example, a simple subroutine to compute the area of a circle:

    SUBROUTINE CIRCLE (X,Y)

    Y = 3.1416 * X ** 2

    RETURN

Clearly, *as far as the subroutine is concerned*, X is the radius of a circle, and Y is its area. How can a programmer use this subroutine? One example might be to code:

Fig. 5.8: *The payroll program with the gross pay subroutine in place.*

```
C     * THIS PROGRAM COMPUTES AND PRINTS  *
C     * AN INDIVIDUAL'S TAKE-HOME PAY.    *
C     *      WRITTEN BY: W.S.DAVIS        *
C     *                  1/10/81          *
C     * * * * * * * * * * * * * * * * * * *

      REAL INCTAX,NETPAY
      CHARACTER*16 NAME
      CHARACTER*2 INIT

C     * THE PROGRAM STARTS BY READING     *
C     * AN INPUT RECORD CONTAINING AN     *
C     * EMPLOYEE'S NAME, INITIALS,        *
C     * HOURS WORKED, AND PAY RATE.       *

   10 READ (5,11,END=99) NAME,INIT,HOURS,RATE

C     * COMPUTE GROSS PAY AND             *
C     * SOCIAL SECURITY TAX.              *

      CALL GROSUB (HOURS,RATE,GROSS)
      SSTAX = GROSS * 0.0665

C     * COMPUTE INCOME TAX.               *

      INCTAX = GROSS * 0.10

C     * COMPUTE NET PAY AND PRINT CHECK;  *
C     * THEN GO BACK AND READ NEXT RECORD.*

      NETPAY = GROSS - (SSTAX + INCTAX)
      WRITE (6,12) NAME,INIT,NETPAY
      GO TO 10

C     * * * * * * * * * * * * * * * * * * *
C     * AT END OF DATA, TERMINATE PROGRAM.*
C     * * * * * * * * * * * * * * * * * * *

   99 STOP
   11 FORMAT (A16,A2,F3.1,F4.2)
   12 FORMAT (5X,A16,'.',A2,3X,'$',F7.2)
      END

      SUBROUTINE GROSUB (HOURS,RATE,GROSS)

C     * * * * * * * * * * * * * * * * * * *
C     * SUBROUTINE TO COMPUTE GROSS PAY.  *
C     * BASE PAY IS THE PRODUCT OF HOURS  *
C     * WORKED AND THE HOURLY PAY RATE.   *
C     * ALL HOURS WORKED OVER 40 ARE PAID *
C     * AT 1.5 TIMES THE REGULAR HOURLY   *
C     * RATE.                             *
C     * * * * * * * * * * * * * * * * * * *

      IF (HOURS .LE. 40.0) THEN DO
         GROSS = HOURS * RATE
      ELSE DO
         GROSS  = 40.0*RATE + (HOURS-40.0)*(RATE*1.5)
      END IF
      RETURN
      END
```

122

```
READ  (5,*)  RADIUS

CALL  CIRCLE  (RADIUS,AREA)

WRITE  (6,*)  AREA
```

The way in which the parameters are passed is illustrated in Fig. 5.9.

The first variable listed after the CALL statement is matched with the first variable in the SUBROUTINE statement; in other words, RADIUS and X now represent the same value. The second variable in the CALL is associated with the second variable in the SUBROUTINE statement—AREA and Y have (or will have) the same value. Very simply, the variables in the CALL statement and the variables in the SUBROUTINE statement are matched, one for one, in the order coded. The data types must match; real variables must be passed to real variables, and integers must be passed to integers. The names may or may not match; it really doesn't matter. Only the order and the data type are significant.

Perhaps it would help if you remember exactly what a FORTRAN variable really is. A FORTRAN variable is simply a name assigned to a storage location. In the example cited above, RADIUS is the name assigned to a storage location that holds a real value in the main program, and AREA is a name assigned to a different storage location that holds a different real number. When the CALL statement is executed and the parameters "passed", all that really happens is that X is identified as another name for the memory location we've been calling RADIUS. In other words, RADIUS is the name of a certain memory location, and X is a sort of nickname or alias. Within the main program, this memory location is known as RADIUS. Within the subroutine, this same memory location is known as X. That's all there is to it.

Fig. 5.9: *Passing parameters.*

```
READ  (5,*)  RADIUS

CALL  CIRCLE  (RADIUS,AREA)
```

```
SUBROUTINE  CIRCLE  (X,Y)

Y = 3.1416 * X ** 2

RETURN
```

Is the programmer restricted to passing variables? No. A constant can be passed too. For example, the statement:

CALL CIRCLE (2.5,AREA)

would cause the subroutine to compute and return the area of a circle with radius 2.5. A constant is simply a known value stored in a known location in memory. In the subroutine, X would refer to this same known location. Note that even when passing constants, the data type must match.

Parameters may be passed in any order; the only requirement is that the order in the CALL statement and the order in the SUBROUTINE statement match. We can, however, make some suggestions. To save yourself from possible confusion, follow a consistent pattern. You might, for example, list the variables or constants being passed *to* the subroutine first, and those being returned *from* the subroutine last. You might list all integers before listing the real parameters. You might list the variables in the order in which they are used in the subroutine. The key idea is that if you have a system, any system, you are much less likely to forget a parameter. In the examples in this book, we will code those parameters being passed to the subroutine first.

A final comment: does the name of a subroutine have anything to do with the subroutine's "type"? For example, is a subroutine whose name begins with "I" limited to the processing of integer variables? *No!* The subroutine name is *not* a concern in determining data type.

A copy of the payroll program with the gross pay subroutine in place was shown in Fig. 5.8. We are now ready to test it. We'll run the program and enter our test data, perhaps the same test data used earlier to test the skeleton mainline. To be certain that everything is working properly, some of that data should be for people who worked more than 40 hours, with other data for people who worked less than 40 hours. For those who worked overtime, the answers should be different from those produced by the skeleton program; for those who didn't, the answers should be the same.

What if the answers are wrong? They were correct before the gross pay subroutine was added. What was changed? Only the gross pay subroutine. Where would we expect to find the error? Clearly, in the gross pay subroutine. The fact that modular program design tends to narrow the search for errors to a single module is one of its most significant advantages.

Eventually, the test data will generate the expected answers. The gross pay subroutine will have passed our test. Thus we'll be ready to add another computational routine to the program.

The Second Subroutine: Income Tax

Social security tax is 6.65% of gross pay, and, except for a condition that we will not consider here, the dummy statement is correct. Thus we turn our attention to the computation of income tax.

Our first task, as always, is to define the problem. We want to compute income tax. How do we do it? What are the rules, the algorithms?

The federal government publishes a book *(Circular E: Employer's Tax Guide)* in which the rules are clearly defined. The specific tax tables are just a bit more complex than we need to illustrate the concepts of this chapter, so we'll make up a simplified table that works in much the same way. Assume that the tax table we are to use is defined as follows:

If gross pay is:	tax is
$0 - $100	10% of gross
$100 - $200	$10 + 20% of gross earnings over $100
$200 and up	$30 + 30% of gross earnings over $100

What if an employee earned $150? For gross pay between $100 and $200, the tax is $10 plus 20 percent of the amount of gross earnings over $100. This excess amount (150 – 100) is $50. Twenty percent of $50 is $10. The tax due is, therefore, $20. Suppose another employee earns $400 in gross pay. This person falls into the highest bracket, paying $30 plus a percentage. The percentage tax would be 30 percent of (400 – 200), which is $60. The base tax is $30. The total tax due is $90.

Now that we understand the income tax algorithm (and the best way to gain such an understanding is to do a few test computations), we can begin to consider the FORTRAN code needed to compute the amount of tax due. The fact that we understand the algorithm does not, however, mean that we know how to code it. Additional planning is necessary.

Logically, how would you use the table to compute tax? The key, of course, is gross pay. Using gross pay, the proper tax bracket can be found, and the tax computed.

The first step might be to compare gross pay with 100, the upper limit of the first bracket. If gross is greater than 100, this employee falls into a higher bracket; if not, we have located the correct bracket and can compute the tax. For those whose gross pay was greater than 100, a comparison against 200, the limit of the second bracket, can be made. Once again, the result of this test can be used to determine if the program will compute the tax using the factors of the second bracket, or move on to the third. This logic is flowcharted in Fig. 5.10.

Now we can write the subroutine (Fig. 5.11). A few comments are in order. Note first the REAL statement immediately following the comments. We plan to use a variable called INCTAX to hold the computed income tax in the subroutine. The income tax is to be a monetary amount correct to the nearest penny; in other words, it must be a real number. What is the default type of a variable named INCTAX? Integer. We can override this default by coding an explicit type statement. Couldn't we have defined data type in the main program? No. Remember that the main program

Fig. 5.10: *Testing to find the proper tax bracket.*

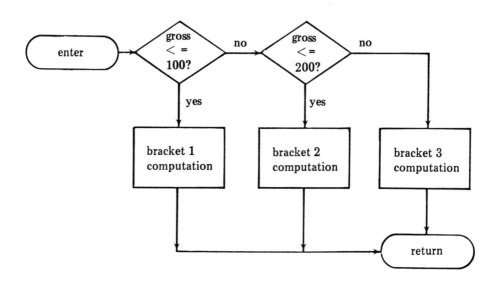

Fig. 5.11: *The income tax subroutine.*

```
      SUBROUTINE FEDTAX (GROSS,INCTAX)
C                              * * * * * * * * * * * * * * * * * *
C                              *  SUBROUTINE TO COMPUTE INCOME TAX.
C                              *  THE TAX RATE CAN BE FOUND BY USING
C                              *  THE COMPUTED GROSS PAY TO SEARCH
C                              *  THE FOLLOWING TABLE:
C                              *     GROSS        TAX
C                              *      0-100      10% OF GROSS
C                              *    100-200      $10 + 20% (GROSS-100)
C                              *    200 AND UP   $30 + 30% (GROSS-200)
C                              * * * * * * * * * * * * * * * * * *
      REAL INCTAX

      IF (GROSS .LE. 100.00) THEN DO
         INCTAX = GROSS * 0.10
      ELSE DO
         IF (GROSS .LE. 200.00) THEN DO
            INCTAX = 10.00 + 0.20*(GROSS-100.00)
         ELSE DO
            INCTAX = 30.00 + 0.30*(GROSS-200.00)
         END IF
      END IF
      RETURN
      END
```

and the subprogram are independent. If a variable is used in a subroutine, its type must be defined in the subroutine.

Note also the structure of the IF. . .THEN. . .ELSE logic block. A condition is tested: Is GROSS less than or equal to 100.00? If the answer is "yes", then income tax is computed at a ten percent rate. If the answer is "no", then another IF test is executed. This is known as a *nested IF*. It is a reasonable way to test two or more related conditions.

The program with two subroutines in place is shown in Fig. 5.12.

Once again, it is time to test the program. The test data should generate gross pay values in each tax bracket; only if each component of a program is tested can we be confident of its accuracy. What if some of the answers are wrong? They were correct before; we added just one function; thus, the error must lie in this new subroutine. As soon as the income tax subroutine has been successfully debugged, we'll be ready to add yet another subroutine.

MODULAR PROGRAM DESIGN

What next? More subroutines can be added. One might take care of the input operation, reading some data, checking the values for reasonability, and making certain that only "good" data are passed to the rest of the program. Routines for state income tax and local income tax might be added. Other subroutines would incorporate other deductions. Additional gross pay complexities can be woven in. The program is likely to be very large and very complex by the time we finish, but, given the step by step approach to design and implementation, it should work. Do you begin to see the value of the modular approach to program design?

The philosophy is simple: take a complex problem, break it into simple problems, and solve each one separately; then put the partial solutions together. If you remember this simple rule, programming is easy. Think first. Then do it.

SUMMARY

The chapter began by discussing the complexity frequently found in real world programming problems. When faced with a complex problem, the programmer will often break it into smaller pieces and then attack the pieces one at a time. This is the essence of a modular approach to program design.

The problem described in the chapter was a payroll program. A hierarchy chart of the program was developed, identifying the major computational modules. Then a skeleton mainline was written and tested. The idea of character variables was introduced.

We then turned our attention to the computational subroutines, writing the logic needed to implement a somewhat more complex gross pay routine and an income tax routine. The subroutines were linked to the mainline by using CALL and RETURN

Fig. 5.12: *The payroll program with the income tax subroutine in place.*

```
C                                          *  THIS PROGRAM COMPUTES AND PRINTS
C                                          *  AN INDIVIDUAL'S TAKE-HOME PAY.
C                                          *      WRITTEN BY: W.S. DAVIS
C                                          *             1/10/81
C                                          *  *  *  *  *  *  *  *  *  *  *  *  *  *  *
      REAL INCTAX,NETPAY
      CHARACTER*16 NAME
      CHARACTER*2  INIT
C                                          *  THE PROGRAM STARTS BY READING
C                                          *  AN INPUT RECORD CONTAINING AN
C                                          *  EMPLOYEE'S NAME, INITIALS,
C                                          *  HOURS WORKED, AND PAY RATE.
C
   10 READ (5,11,END=99) NAME,INIT,HOURS,RATE
C
C                                          *  COMPUTE GROSS PAY AND
C                                          *  SOCIAL SECURITY TAX.
      CALL GROSUB (HOURS,RATE,GROSS)
      SSTAX = GROSS * 0.0665
C                                          *  COMPUTE INCOME TAX.
      CALL FEDTAX (GROSS,INCTAX)
C                                          *  COMPUTE NET PAY AND PRINT CHECK;
C                                          *  THEN GO BACK AND READ NEXT RECORD.
C
      NETPAY = GROSS - (SSTAX + INCTAX)
      WRITE (6,12) NAME,INIT,NETPAY
      GO TO 10
C                                          *  *  *  *  *  *  *  *  *  *  *  *  *  *  *
C                                          *  AT END OF DATA, TERMINATE PROGRAM.*
C                                          *  *  *  *  *  *  *  *  *  *  *  *  *  *  *
   99 STOP
   11 FORMAT (A16,A2,F3.1,F4.2)
   12 FORMAT (5X,A16,',',A2,3X,'$',F7.2)
      END
C    -----------------------------------------------------------------------------

      SUBROUTINE GROSUB (HOURS,RATE,GROSS)
C                                          *  *  *  *  *  *  *  *  *  *  *  *  *  *  *
C                                          *  SUBROUTINE TO COMPUTE GROSS PAY.
C                                          *  BASE PAY IS THE PRODUCT OF HOURS
C                                          *  WORKED AND THE HOURLY PAY RATE.
C                                          *  ALL HOURS WORKED OVER 40 ARE PAID
C                                          *  AT 1.5 TIMES THE REGULAR HOURLY
C                                          *  RATE.
C                                          *  *  *  *  *  *  *  *  *  *  *  *  *  *  *
      IF (HOURS .LE. 40.0) THEN DO
         GROSS = HOURS * RATE
      ELSE DO
         GROSS = 40.0*RATE + (HOURS-40.0)*(RATE*1.5)
      END IF
      RETURN
      END

      SUBROUTINE FEDTAX (GROSS,INCTAX)
C                                          *  *  *  *  *  *  *  *  *  *  *  *  *  *  *
C                                          *  SUBROUTINE TO COMPUTE INCOME TAX.
C                                          *  THE TAX RATE CAN BE FOUND BY USING
C                                          *  THE COMPUTED GROSS PAY TO SEARCH
C                                          *  THE FOLLOWING TABLE:
C                                          *     GROSS       TAX
C                                          *     0-100       10% OF GROSS
C                                          *     100-200     $10 + 20% (GROSS-100)
C                                          *     200 AND UP  $30 + 30% (GROSS-200)
C                                          *  *  *  *  *  *  *  *  *  *  *  *  *  *  *
      REAL INCTAX

      IF (GROSS .LE. 100.00) THEN DO
         INCTAX = GROSS * 0.10
      ELSE DO
         IF (GROSS .LE. 200.00) THEN DO
            INCTAX = 10.00 + 0.20*(GROSS-100.00)
         ELSE DO
            INCTAX = 30.00 + 0.30*(GROSS-200.00)
         END IF
      END IF
      RETURN
      END
```

statements. The chapter closed with a few comments on the value of the modular approach to program design.

EXERCISES

1. Assume that a new union contract calls for a shift premium of 10% to be added to the gross pay of all employees working the second shift. According to the contract, gross pay is to be computed as before, and then, if the employee works second shift, this 10% premium is to be added. How would you modify the chapter program to include this new feature? Would you have to add anything to the READ statement? Make the necessary changes and run the program.

2. Assume that the people working for our firm live in three different areas: city A, city B, and city C. Each city has a local income tax, charging the following rates:

City	Rate
A	1.0%
B	0.5%
C	1.5%

    Add a subroutine (and necessary linkage) to the payroll program to compute local income tax; don't forget to consider this deduction in computing net pay. Once again, you may have to add something to input. What?

3. Many states have a state income tax. If your state does, get a tax withholding table (try your school's payroll department) and add a subroutine to the payroll program to compute this tax.

4. Add a subroutine to compute union dues. The rule is: if gross pay is less than $150, dues are $2.50; otherwise, dues are $5.00.

5. Modify the income tax subroutine of the chapter payroll program to consider the following factor. Tax should not be computed based on the amount of gross pay. Instead, the basis for entering the table should be taxable income, which is computed by subtracting from gross pay $7.50 for each dependent (child, spouse, etc.) claimed. What changes must be made to input? Be careful in your computations; it is possible to have a negative taxable income.

6. Write a program to compute and print performance statistics for a baseball team. Input data will be as follows:

Hitters	Pitchers
number	number
name	name
times at bat	innings pitched
hits	earned runs
H, for hitter	P, for pitcher

Your program should read the input record and determine the player's position from the code (H for hitter, P for pitcher). For all hitters, link to a subroutine and compute the batting average, which is defined as:

$$AVERAGE = HITS / AT BATS$$

For all pitchers, compute the earned run average, which is defined as:

$$ERA = RUNS / (INNINGS/9);$$

once again, use a subroutine. Following computations, print the player's number, name, and other relevant data.

7. Chapter 3, problem 5 asked you to write a program to compute the factorial of an integer. Chapter 4, problem 16 used factorials in computing (or estimating) a sin. Redo the latter problem, writing a subroutine to compute a factorial.

8. In statistics and probability, it is often necessary to compute the number of different possible outcomes of an event. By computing the number of combinations or permutations, it is sometimes possible to find this number of different possible outcomes. For "n" things taken "r" at a time, the formula for combinations is:

$$\frac{n!}{r!\,(n-r)!}$$

and the formula for permuations is

$$\frac{n!}{(n-r)!}$$

where n! is "n factorial".

Write a program to read a value for n and a value for r and compute the number of combinations and permutations possible. Note that r must be less than n. Since several factorials must be computed, it is strongly recommended that you code the factorial routine as a subroutine.

9. Write a program to generate electric bills. Input to the program will consist of a rate code, a user number, and the number of kilowatt hours used. Develop a skeleton mainline first. The rate charged for electricity is based on the rate code. In the skeleton mainline, use the following simplified rate table:

Code	Meaning	Rate
1	Regular household	2½ cents/kilowatt hour
2	Total electricity	2 cents/kilowatt hour
3	Factory	1½ cents/kilowatt hour
4	Non-profit	1 cent/kilowatt hour

The skeleton mainline should read an input record, determine the proper rate by checking the rate code, compute the bill from the skeleton formula, and print the customer number, the number of kilowatt hours used, and the amount of the bill. Be sure to include test data for each of the four rates.

10. Modify the program of exercise 9, adding a subroutine to compute the actual electric bill for a regular household (rate code = 1), using the following table:

Base charge	$3.00
First 1000 kilowatt hrs	2.49 cents per kilowatt hour
Additional kilowatt hrs	1.60 cents per kilowatt hour
Fuel adjustment	1.6399 cents per kilowatt hour

Note that the base charge is added to the bill no matter how many kilowatt hours are used; in other words, even if the usage is zero, the charge is a minimum of $3.00. If usage is greater than zero, the charge is $3.00 plus the charge per kilowatt hour. The fuel adjustment is an extra charge of *all* kilowatt hours used.

11. Add subroutines for other rate codes, using the following rules:

Code	Base Charge	Charge/kilowatt after				Fuel Adj.
		0	1000	2000	5000	
2	$ 3.00	2.49 cents	1.60 cents	1.25 cents	1.25 cents	1.6399 cents
3	$50.00	0	0	1.00 cents	0.75 cents	1.6399 cents
4	$ 5.00	1.25 cents	1.25 cents	0.75 cents	0.75 cents	1.6399 cents

12. Loan officers in a bank often find it necessary to do interest computations. Among the questions they must answer are:

a. If I invest P dollars today, at i% interest, how much will I have after n years? The formula is:

$$F = P(1+i)^n$$

b. I want to have F dollars n years from now. How much must I invest today at i% interest? The formula is:

$$P = F/(1+i)^n$$

c. If I deposit R dollars each year for n years, how much will I have (at i% interest)? The formula is:

$$F = R\frac{(1+i)^n - 1}{i}$$

d. I need F dollars in n years. How much must I invest each year at i% interest? The formula is:

$$R = F\frac{i}{(1+i)^n - 1}$$

e. If I borrow P dollars today for n years, how much must I repay each year at i% interest? The formula is:

$$R = P\frac{i(1+i)^n}{(1+i)^n - 1}$$

f. How much is a promise to pay R dollars per year for n years at i% interest worth today? The formula is:

$$P = R \frac{(1+i)^n - 1}{i(1+i)^n}$$

Write a program to input a code identifying the interest computation to be performed (A, B, C, D, E, or F). Then input a dollar amount (either P, F, or R depending on the computation to be performed), the interest rate, and the number of years. The six interest computation formulas should be located in six computational subroutines; link to the proper subroutine and do the computations. Then print the input values and the computed answer. Don't forget to clearly identify your results.

13. Simulation is a most interesting application of the computer. As an elementary simulation exercise, write a program to simulate the rolling of a pair of dice.

The secret to simulating is the use of random numbers. The FORTRAN subroutine RANDU can be used to generate a random number between 0 and 1. It is coded as:

CALL RANDU (IX,IY,YFL)

where IX is an integer "seed", IY is the seed you should use the next time you CALL RANDU, and YFL is the random number. A single die has six surfaces numbered 1 through 6. We can simulate the result of rolling that die. Since RANDU returns a value between 0 and 1, we can get 1, 2, 3, 4, 5, or 6 by coding:

N = INT (YFL * 6 + 1)

Multiplying the value returned by YFL by 6 yields a value between 0 and 6; in other words, the value is greater than 0 but less than 6. Adding 1 gives us a number greater than 1 but less than 7. Taking the integer portion of this number (the INT function) drops the fractional portion leaving only the whole number—the result will be 1, 2, 3, 4, 5, or 6.

Your program should begin by generating two rolls of a single die. Print the two values and their sum. Place the routine that generates random numbers between 1 and 6 in a subroutine.

Once you have written this skeleton program, you may want to add some "bells and whistles" of your own. Consider, for example, the logic needed to allow a single player to bet against the computer. Consider dice games involving multiple players. Consider implementing the rules of craps. As you extend your program, don't forget to use subroutines for introducing new functions.

14. There are 52 cards in a deck. Assign the number 1 through 4 to the aces, 5 through 8 to the kings, and so on. Generate random numbers between 1 and 52; simply multiply YFL (from RANDU) by 52, add 1, and take the integer portion.

Write a program to play a game of acey/duecy or high/low. Use your random number function to select two cards. The player then bets. If the next card lies between the first two, the player wins; if not, the computer wins. Use subroutines for the random number function and to figure out the value of the card. You might also consider using a subroutine to keep track of the player's winnings and losings.

6

Arrays

In a typical program, data is input, processed, and then the results are output. A second cycle of the program involves a different set of data. Each data element is used once, and does not impact subsequent repetitions of the program.

Occasionally, the programmer will encounter a problem where the same data is needed more than once. The option of retyping is always available, of course, but retyping is time-consuming and error prone. It is much better to enter the data once and store it in the computer. Once the data have been stored, they can be used as often as is necessary.

In this chapter, we will consider such a problem. An array will be used to hold the data.

135

STANDARDIZED TEST SCORING

Is there any student in the United States who has never taken a standardized test? Probably not. With IQ tests, interest tests, achievement tests, and college entrance examinations, most students have been exposed to several.

The scores earned on such tests are a bit unusual. An IQ test uses 100 as the average. College board scores range from a low of 200 to a high of 800; on the ACT test, scores range from 0 to 30. What is a "passing" score? There isn't any! In fact, that is the point. Standardized tests are not designed to generate grades on an A, B, C scale. Instead, they are designed to rank a student with respect to others who took the same test. It is this relative ranking that is important, and not some arbitrary grading scheme. Designers of standardized tests go out of their way to report scores that are difficult to convert to traditional grades.

Imagine that we have been assigned the task of writing a program to compute and print the scores on such an exam. We will use as our model the SAT (Scholastic Aptitude Test). Each student's score is to fall between 200 and 800, with an average of 500. How might we go about developing such a program?

DESIGNING THE ALGORITHM

The first step is to very clearly define the algorithm or algorithms involved in computing a score. It's one thing to state that scores should lie between 200 and 400, with an average of 500. It is quite different to define *precisely* how such scores are to be computed.

Each student who takes the exam earns a *raw score*, the number of questions answered correctly. Often, to adjust for random guessing, a factor based on the number of questions answered incorrectly is used, but the raw score essentially measures a student's correct answers.

The key to converting raw scores into relative scores on a 200-800 scale is the *average raw score*; add the raw scores of all the students, divide by the number of students, and you have the average. If your score is *exactly* equal to the average, you should earn a 500; if you did better than average, you should earn more than 500; if you did worse, your examination score will be below 500. The rule we will use (which may not be exactly the same as that used by the people at Educational Testing Service) is:

$$\text{Exam score} = \frac{\text{student raw score}}{\text{average raw score}} * 500$$

An average raw score will generate an exam score of 500. An above average raw score yields an exam score greater than 500. If the raw score is below average, the ratio (student raw/average raw) must be less than 1, so the computed score must be less than 500.

Consider, for example, the following three students:

Student	Raw Score	Raw/Average	Exam Score
Aaron	150	1.5	750
Baker	100	1.0	500
Cooper	50	0.5	250

The raw scores are, respectively, 150, 100, and 50. The average raw score (sum the three and divide by 3) is 100. Aaron's ratio is thus 150/100, which is 1.5; Baker's ratio is 100/100, which is 1.0; Cooper's is 50/100, which is 0.5. Multiplying each ratio by 500 generates the scores shown in the rightmost column.

How can we make certain that all the scores lie between 200 and 800? If the computed examination score is greater than 800, it is made equal to 800, and if the score is less than 200, it is made equal to 200. That, basically, completes the algorithm.

THE PROBLEM: THE DATA MUST BE USED TWICE

There is only one problem with this algorithm: the input data must be used *twice*. How is the average raw score computed? Each input raw score must be read, counted, and accumulated. How are the individual examination scores computed? Each raw score must be compared with the average raw score. Obviously, the average raw score must be known before any of the individual examination scores can be computed. *All* the data must be used to find the average, and then *all* the data must be used *again* to compute individual scores.

It is possible, of course, to input the data twice. As long as there is only a tiny amount of data, this might be reasonable, but if a significant amount of data must be entered, inputting it twice would be both time-consuming and error prone. There must be a better way. There must be a way to enter the data once, store it within the computer, and then use it again as necessary. There is. We can store the data in an array.

ARRAYS

Assume that we will be reading a total of 25 raw scores. How can we store all these scores in the computer? One alternative might be to define 25 different variables: RAW01 through RAW25, for example. We could then:

        READ (5,*) RAW01,RAW02,RAW03, . . . and so on.

Later, we could sum these values by coding:

        ACCUM = RAW01 + RAW02 + RAW03 + . . . and so on.

Finally, each variable could be divided by the computed average raw score to get the examination scores, a series of 25 assignment statements!

Imagine keeping track of all those variables. Now imagine the same problem with 50 scores. 100! Ridiculous. Once again, there must be a better way. Twenty-five values require twenty-five storage locations. If each value is to be used independently (and it must be), then each storage location must have a unique name. However, the twenty-five raw scores are not really all that different; they are different values of the *same* statistic. They are related. Often, the best way to handle such data is to define an array.

Defining an Array

An array is simply a series of consecutive memory locations. It is defined by coding a **DIMENSION** statement. Consider, for example, the comparison sketched in Fig. 6.1. On the left is the space assigned to the variable X; it consists of a single memory location (on most systems, a single *word*). On the right is the space assigned to the array defined by:

DIMENSION Y(4)

It consists of four consecutive memory locations. (The number in parentheses defines the number of elements in the array.)

How do we differentiate between these four memory locations? We use subscripts. The first location in the array is Y(1), or Y-sub-1. The element is Y(2), the third is Y(3), and so on. The subscript is nothing more than the number of the element in the array.

Using an Array

An array element can be used just like any regular variable. For example, the statement:

Y(1) = 15.0

would initialize the first element in the array to the value 15, while:

Y(2) = 0.0

would set the second element to zero.

We can also use subscripted variables in a READ statement. The statement:

READ (5,*) Y(1), Y(2), Y(3), Y(4)

might be used to allow the programmer to provide, through an input card or a terminal, initial values for each of the array elements.

Variable X   DIMENSION Y(4)

Y(1)

Y(2)

Y(3)

Y(4)

The subscript need not, however, be a constant; we can use a variable instead. Consider, for example, the following loop:

DO 40 N = 1,4

READ (5,*) Y(N)

40 CONTINUE

Assuming that an array named Y had been created by an earlier DIMENSION statement, this loop could be used to initialize the array. In Fig. 6.2, the process of filling the array is illustrated step by step. As the loop begins, N is set equal to 1 (Fig. 6.2a). The READ statement is executed. As the first number comes into the computer, N is equal to 1. Thus Y(N) is really Y(1). The value is stored at memory location Y(1).

The second time through the loop (Fig. 6.2b), the value of N will be 2. Once again the READ statement will be executed. As this second value goes into the computer, N is 2. Thus Y(N) really means Y(2). The second value is stored at memory location Y(2).

The third time through, N will be 3. Thus the value will be stored at location Y(3)—see Fig. 6.2c. This process continues (Fig. 6.2d) until the loop ends.

Fig. 6.2: *Filling an array (a).*

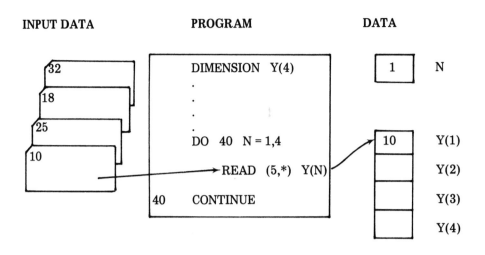

Fig. 6.2: *Filling an array (b).*

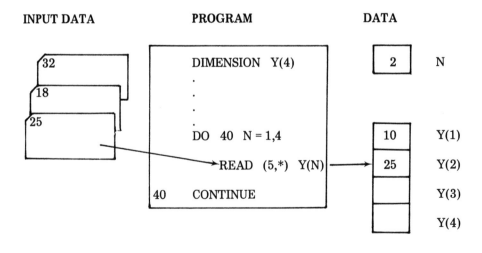

Fig. 6.2: *Filling an array (c).*

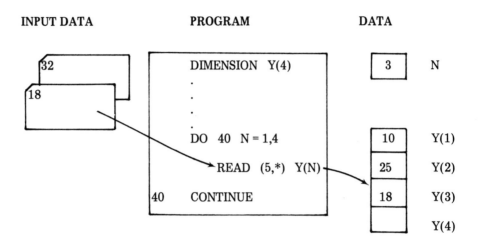

Fig. 6.2: *Filling an array (d).*

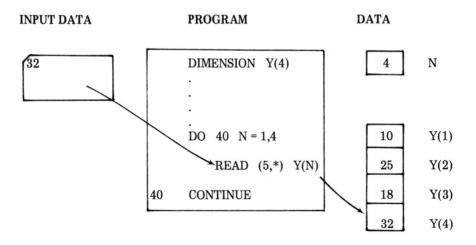

Can the elements in an array be used in an assignment statement? Yes. Consider, for example, the loop:

DO 60 N = 1,4

ACCUM = ACCUM + Y(N)

60 CONTINUE

This loop would accumulate all the elements of the array.

USING AN ARRAY IN THE EXAMINATION SCORING PROBLEM

Earlier in the chapter, we developed an algorithm for an examination scoring problem. The input data was needed twice: once to compute the average raw score, and again to compute the individual examination scores. Using an array is an excellent way to handle this problem. Initially, the data can be read into an array. Once in, the array elements can be summed as part of the "average computation" logic. Later, the same array elements can be used to compute the individual scores.

How would we structure such a program? A number of steps are involved. The problem can become quite lengthy and thus quite complex. As was the case in Chapter 5, when we are faced with a potentially complex problem, the best strategy is often to break it into relatively simple modules. We can identify three such modules in this program; they are (Fig. 6.3):

1. fill the array,

2. compute the average raw score,

3. compute and print the individual exam scores.

Clearly, we must have the data before we can compute the average, and we must have the average before we can compute the examination scores; thus our modular view of the program defines sequence.

What is it that ties these three basic modules together? The data. Module 1 fills the array; modules 2 and 3 use the data in the array. Module 2 computes the average; module 3 uses the computed average. Except for these data elements, the three modules are independent, so we can code them independently, and put the pieces together later. We must, however, first agree on the data names. We'll define an array named RAW (for RAW scores), using the following statement:

DIMENSION RAW(25)

The computed average will be AVG. We can now begin planning and writing the program logic.

Fig. 6.3: *The structure of the examination scoring program.*

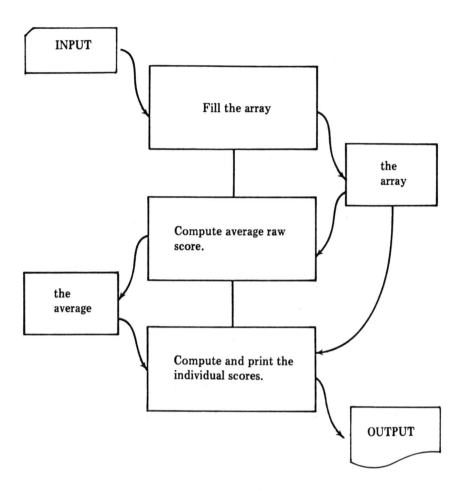

The "Table Fill" Module

The first module fills the table. The logic is simple (Fig. 6.4): input a series of values within a loop, and assign each to the "next" array element. The FORTRAN code is, in this case, simplier than the flowchart (Fig. 6.5); all we need is a DO loop containing a READ statement. We'll assume that there are exactly 25 raw scores to be entered.

The "Compute Average" Module

The table is now full, and we can move on to the next bit of logic. How do we compute an average? All the elements in the table must be summed, and this sum must be divided by the number of elements, in this case, 25. The logic is outlined in Fig. 6.6, the code is shown in Fig. 6.7.

Fig. 6.4: *The "table fill" logic.*

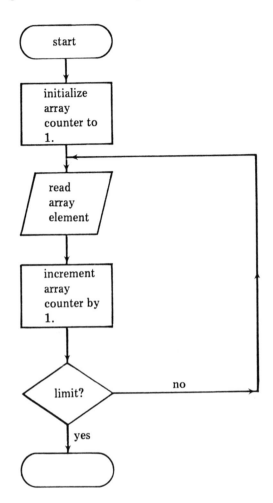

Fig. 6.5: *FORTRAN code for the "table fill" logic.*

```
C
C
C
C
C
C
          DIMENSION RAW(25)
          DO 50 N=1,25
             READ. RAW(N)
       50 CONTINUE
```

```
    *   PROGRAM TO COMPUTE EXAMINATION
    *   SCORES FOR A NUMBER OF STUDENTS.
    *      WRITTEN BY: W.S. DAVIS
    *                    1/10/81
    * * * * * * * * * * * * * * * * *
    *   THE FIRST STEP IS TO FILL A
    *   TABLE WITH RAW SCORES.
```

Fig. **6.6**: *The logic of the "compute average" module.*

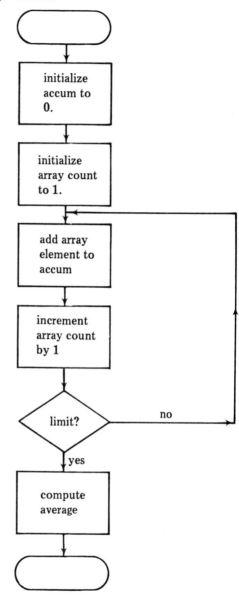

Fig. **6.7**: *The FORTRAN code for the "compute average" module.*

```
C                                            * NEXT, THE AVERAGE RAW SCORE
C                                            * IS COMPUTED.
        ACCUM = 0.0
        DO 60 N=1,25
            ACCUM = ACCUM + RAW(N)
     60 CONTINUE
        AVG = ACCUM/25.0
```

145

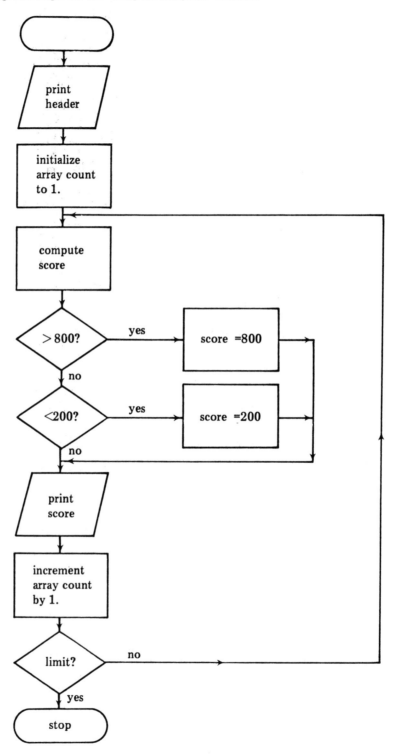

The "Compute and Print" Module

Once the average raw score has been computed, we can enter the last phase of the program and compute and print the individual examination scores. Following the printing of a set of headers and the initialization of an array counter to 1, we enter the loop and compute a student's score. Next, we must test to make certain that the limits of 800 and 200 are met. Finally, the computed score can be printed, the array counter (really, the subscript) incremented by 1, and the loop repeated until all the computations have been completed.

Examination scores are to be printed as whole numbers, with no fractional part. Real numbers have a fractional part. Thus we use the variable ISAT to hold the computed score (Fig. 6.9). You should have little trouble following the logic.

The Complete Program

The time has come to put the pieces together and form a complete program (Fig. 6.10). The program is relatively long and fairly complex. Had we attacked it as a single, large program, we might have encountered difficulty. We decided, however, to break it into pieces. Instead of writing one large program, we wrote three small ones. A potentially difficult task was greatly simplified.

Fig. 6.9: *The FORTRAN code for the "compute and print" module.*

```
C                                         *  GIVEN THE RAW SCORES AND THE
C                                         *  COMPUTED AVERAGE RAW SCORE. THE
C                                         *  STUDENT'S EXAMINATION SCORE CAN
C                                         *  BE COMPUTED FROM THE FORMULA
C                                         *     SAT = (RAW/AVG RAW)*500
C                                         *  USING THIS FORMULA. THE AVERAGE
C                                         *  SCORE WILL BE 500. ADDITIONAL
C                                         *  TESTS WILL BE USED TO ENSURE
C                                         *  THAT THE MAXIMUM SCORE WILL BE
C                                         *  800 AND THE MINIMUM WILL BE 200.
C                                         *  THE FINAL SCORE WILL BE SHOWN TO
C                                         *  ITS NEAREST INTEGER VALUE.
      WRITE (6,11)
      DO 70 N=1,25
         ISAT = (RAW(N)/AVG)*500.0
         IF (ISAT .GT. 800) THEN DO
            ISAT = 800
         ELSE DO
            IF (ISAT .LT. 200) THEN DO
               ISAT = 200
            ELSE DO
            END IF
         END IF
         WRITE (6,12) N,RAW(N),ISAT
70    CONTINUE
      STOP
11    FORMAT ('1',T10,'STUDENT',T20,'RAW SCORE',T30,'SAT SCORE')
12    FORMAT (T13,I2,T23,F4.0,T33,I3)
      END
```

147

Is there room for improvement? Of course! For example, it might be possible to combine the loop that reads values and fills the table, with the loop that accumulates the values, thus saving several steps. It would certainly be desirable to generalize this program so that it does not assume *exactly* 25 input values. By adding a counter to the first loop, exiting the first loop when a critical condition (such as a $EOJ card or a negative raw score) was encountered, and then using the count as the upper limit on subsequent loops, the program would be capable of dealing with any number of raw scores (up to the limit imposed by the size of the array). The time for such attention to detail is now, *after* the logic has been carefully defined. Efficient code is irrelevant if the answers are wrong.

SUMMARY

In this chapter, we developed a program to compute scores on a standardized test modelled after the Scholastic Aptitude Test. The key problem arose from the fact that the data, raw scores, were used twice, once to compute the average raw score and again to compute the individual examination scores.

To solve the problem of multiple use of the data, we defined an array by using a DIMENSION statement. An array is a series of related main memory locations. By using subscripts, the elements contained in the array can be uniquely identified.

We identified three primary functions the program would have to perform: fill the array, compute the average, and compute the individual scores. We then wrote the code for each function independently, putting the pieces together after defining the logic—a modular approach to programming.

EXERCISES

1. Generalize the text example so that it accepts any number (up to a limit of 50) of raw scores and computes and prints the associated examination scores.

2. Add to the text example the logic needed to input the student's name and, later, to print the name along with the raw score and the examination score. Note: a character array can be defined by coding CHARACTER * 16 NAME(25), or a similar instruction.

3. In a different standardized test, the algorithm for computing a score begins with the computation of an average raw score. However, the final scores are to be generated with an average of 18, a maximum of 30, and a minimum of 0. Write a program to read the raw scores and compute individual examination scores using this new algorithm.

4. Write a program to generate a multiplication table. Use an array of ten elements to set up a series of computations in main memory (5*1, 5*2, 5*3, and so on,

Fig. 6.10: *The complete examination scoring program.*

```
C     * PROGRAM TO COMPUTE EXAMINATION
C     * SCORES FOR A NUMBER OF STUDENTS.
C     *      WRITTEN BY: W.S. DAVIS
C     *                  1/10/81
C     * * * * * * * * * * * * * * * *
C     * THE FIRST STEP IS TO FILL A
C     * TABLE WITH RAW SCORES.

      DIMENSION RAW(25)
      DO 50 N=1,25
      READ, RAW(N)
   50 CONTINUE

C     * NEXT, THE AVERAGE RAW SCORE
C     * IS COMPUTED.

      ACCUM = 0.0
      DO 60 N=1,25
      ACCUM = ACCUM + RAW(N)
   60 CONTINUE
      AVG = ACCUM/25.0

C     * GIVEN THE RAW SCORES AND THE
C     * COMPUTED AVERAGE RAW SCORE, THE
C     * STUDENT'S EXAMINATION SCORE CAN
C     * BE COMPUTED FROM THE FORMULA
C     * SAT = (RAW/AVG RAW)*500
C     * USING THIS FORMULA, THE AVERAGE
C     * SCORE WILL BE 500. ADDITIONAL
C     * TESTS WILL BE USED TO ENSURE
C     * THAT THE MAXIMUM SCORE WILL BE
C     * 800 AND THE MINIMUM WILL BE 200.
C     * THE FINAL SCORE WILL BE SHOWN TO
C     * ITS NEAREST INTEGER VALUE.

      WRITE (6,11)
      DO 70 N=1,25
      ISAT = (RAW(N)/AVG)*500.0
      IF (ISAT .GT. 800) THEN DO
      ISAT = 800
      ELSE DO
      IF (ISAT .LT. 200) THEN DO
      ISAT = 200
      ELSE DO
      END IF
      END IF
      WRITE (6,12) N,RAW(N),ISAT
   70 CONTINUE
      STOP
   11 FORMAT ('1',T10,'STUDENT',T20,'RAW SCORE',T30,'SAT SCORE')
   12 FORMAT (T13,I2,T23,F4.0,T33,I3)
      END
```

149

for example). Then print the array. In the next loop, compute the multiplication table for the next integer (the 6-times table, for example), and print it.

After you have completed this program, look into the use of 2-dimensional arrays on your system. Revise the program to set up a *complete* multiplication table in memory (1-times through 10-times) before printing or displaying the table.

5. Revise the wind chill factor program of Chapter 4. Set up an array of five elements to hold the computed wind chill factors for a constant temperature and for wind velocities ranging from 10 to 50 miles per hour. Print all five values on a single line. The objective is to print a table, with the wind velocity going across the top and the temperature going down the side, such as:

WIND VELOCITY-MPH

TEMP	10	20	30	40	50
-30	—	—	—	—	—
-20	—	—	—	—	—

and so on.

6. Use arrays to generate a similar table (to the one described in exercise 5) for the temperature/humidity index described in Chapter 4, exercise 17.

7. Write a program to read ten or more values (in random order) into an array. Search the array and find the largest value. Search the array again and find the smallest value. Print the largest value, the smallest value, and their difference.

8. Revise exercise 7 to fill and search a character array.

9. An automobile dealership employes ten salespeople. Each year, a competition is held. The employee who sells the most cars is identified, as is the employee who sells the fewest cars. The high salesperson is paid a bonus of $10 per car for the difference between his or her sales and those of the low salesperson. The low salesperson is assigned to the used car lot for the next year. Sales statistics by month for the past year were as follows:

Person	J	F	M	A	M	J	J	A	S	O	N	D
1	12	7	7	4	4	0	9	5	0	9	4	6
2	0	9	2	11	9	5	3	9	4	5	5	7
3	5	1	6	6	8	7	8	0	5	12	6	5
4	3	10	15	6	1	9	6	3	4	9	5	3
5	4	7	7	5	7	4	15	2	5	3	1	9
6	9	2	2	5	3	5	12	16	13	0	5	5
7	8	0	6	8	9	3	6	2	3	1	7	5
8	8	0	0	5	4	9	4	2	2	7	8	2
9	8	2	4	2	8	3	3	2	0	6	8	5
10	6	5	7	4	9	8	0	8	6	3	7	6

HINT: define one input record for each salesperson. Set up an array. READ the sales statistics and accumulate the monthly sales for each salesperson; place these accumulated totals in the array. Look at exercise 7 for a hint as to how to continue.

10. Read at least ten values into an array. The input data should be in random order. Sort it.

11. Two common statistical computations are the mean and standard deviation of a set of data points. If we call our data points:

$$X_1, X_2, X_3, \ldots X_n$$

the mean can be defined as:

$$\bar{X} = \frac{\sum_{i=1}^{n} X_i}{n}$$

or: X-bar is equal to the sum of all the individual values of X divided by the number of different values. Standard deviation is defined as:

$$s = \sqrt{\dfrac{\displaystyle\sum_{i=1}^{n}(X_i - X)^2}{n - 1}}$$

In English this means:

    a. Subtract the computed mean (X) from each individual value of X and square the result.

    b. Sum these individual results for all values of X.

    c. Divide this sum by n, the number of values, minus 1.

    d. Take the square root of this result.

Write a program to compute these two statistics from input data consisting of at least 10 data points.

12. At some point in your education, an instructor has undoubtedly shown you a frequency distribution of grades something like the following:

Grade Range	Number of Students
90 and above	5
80-89	8
70-79	12
60-69	8
59 and below	5

By so grouping the data, the instructor (not to mention the student) gets a very clear picture of where each student stands with respect to the rest of the class. The use of frequency distributions is not, of course, limited to the field of education, being commonly used in business, government and other fields to group and clarify such data as: salary levels, order status, product quality, production rate, sales results, population statistics, and many other types of data too numerous to mention.

The field of statistics uses several terms to describe a frequency distribution. In this sample distribution shown above, we have five *classes*: 90 and above, 80-89, 70-79, 60-69, and 59 and below; each class is a single logical grouping of data. The *class interval* is ten; i.e., each class contains ten possible values. The *class limits* are 90 and below 60; these represent the initial value of the top and bottom "open ended" classes.

Other arrangements are possible. Let's say, for example, we were to specify an *upper* class limit of 95, a class interval of 5, and a total of 11 classes. The resulting classes would be:

95 and above
90-94
85-89
80-84
75-79
70-74
65-69
60-64
55-59
50-54
49 and below

Write a program to generate a frequency distribution. Your program should READ the upper (or lower) class limit, the class interval, and the number of classes. Run the program at least twice, using different frequency distribution parameters. READ the parameters first; then READ the data.

13. Sales records for the past month show that our three salespeople sold the following amounts of our four basic products:

		Product			
		A	B	C	D
	1	14	24	3	57
Salesperson	2	7	17	8	35
	3	22	20	5	32

Product selling prices are:

Product	Unit Price
A	$10.50
B	$15.55
C	$25.00
D	$ 5.95

Write a program to read each salesperson's record and print a sales report consisting of the following information:

SALESPERSON	PRODUCT A		PRODUCT B		PRODUCT C		PRODUCT D		TOTAL
	QUANTITY	REVENUE	QUANTITY	REVENUE	QUANTITY	REVENUE	QUANTITY	REVENUE	REVENUE

Revenue is defined as the product of quantity and unit price. Use one DATA statement for each salesperson's record. Use one or more arrays to hold the sales statistics.

14. A speciality shop stocks ten items. The current stock on hand for each of the ten items is as follows:

Item No.	Quantity
1	14
2	28
3	3
4	95
5	12
6	37
7	18
8	9
9	42
10	11

During the current week, all part numbers had activity as follows:

DAY	ITEM	CODE	QUANT.
M	2	2	5
M	5	2	10
M	9	2	23
T	2	2	15
T	1	2	10
T	4	2	15
T	5	2	2
W	8	1	25
W	7	2	8
W	3	1	25
W	7	2	8
T	3	2	12
T	6	2	10
T	8	2	20
F	1	1	25
F	10	2	3
F	4	2	32
F	6	2	10
F	7	1	25

Each transaction should be represented by a separate input record, with a code of "1" meaning an addition to inventory, and a code of "2" meaning a deletion from inventory.

Initialize an array to hold the current level of inventory for each item; READ the complete "old inventory" at the start of your program. Read individual transactions, keeping track of additions and deletions by item number. HINT: Use the item number as your subscript.

Print a report showing: Beginning inventory, the sum of all additions to inventory, the sum of all deletions from inventory, and ending inventory. Place an asterisk (*) to the right of the ending inventory field for any part number having an ending inventory less than ten (10)—this is a reorder flag. Use explicit column headings.

15. READ a series of grades (in random order) ranging from a low of 40 to a high of 100 into an array. Count the number of grades in the 90s, the 80s, the 70s, the 60s, and below 60. Print the counts.

16. Add to the payroll program of Chapter 5 a new subroutine to compute the amount of local tax due. Local tax varies with the employee's place of residence. We have defined the following city codes and associated percentage rates:

CITY	RATE
1	1.5%
2	1.0%
3	0.5%
4	0.75%
5	0.25%
6	1.25%

At the start of your program, link to a new subroutine that fills a local tax rate array from a series of input records containing these percentages. Within the mainline of your program, include a variable for city code as part of your statement. Link to a new subroutine that searches the table by the city code and computes local tax (a percentage of gross pay).

17. An earlier exercise, number 12, asked you to write a program to generate a frequency distribution. Your output consisted of a series of numbers, one for each class.

Modify the program to print a bar chart of the distribution. For example, the sample data in exercise 12 was:

Grade range	Number of students
90 and above	5
80-89	8
70-79	12
60-69	8
below 60	5

A bar chart to represent this distribution might be:

```
90 and above   *****
80-89          *******
70-79          ***********
60-69          *******
below 60       *****
```

with one asterisk (*) for each student in a given range.

Hint: Set up a character array to hold several 1-character fields. Use the count for a given range to determine how many asterisks will be moved into the array; blank the rest of the array. Now, print the array on a single line.

Module D

More on Arrays

The skilled programmer can do a great deal with arrays. In business programming, various tables can be set up and used. In computational or scientific programming, the rules of linear algebra can be used to manipulate arrays. If you become serious about programming, you will almost certainly find yourself using arrays. This module presents a bit more detail on FORTRAN arrays.

A FEW CODING RULES

1. Always code your DIMENSION statements *before* referencing an element in the array. In fact, it is a good idea to code *all* your DIMENSION statements at the beginning of the program, following your comments and preceeding any executable code.

2. You must define the type of a variable *before* defining it as an array. For example, the sequence:

    DIMENSION NUMBER(50)   *Note: this code is incorrect.*

    REAL NUMBER

    is *wrong*. Given this sequence, an array of 50 integer values would be set up, and *then* the compiler would discover that NUMBER was to be treated as REAL. Code the type statement first, as in:

    REAL NUMBER

    DIMENSION NUMBER(50)

3. It is possible to define variable type *and* an array in a single explicit type statement. Simply code:

    REAL NUMBER(50)

    or:

    INTEGER N(25),VALUES(45)

4. Do *not* use the same name for both an array and a regular variable. Such use is illegal on most versions of FORTRAN. Even if your compiler allows you to refer to X(1) and X in the same program, don't; it's bad coding practice.

5. The lower bound on subscripts is 1 on most systems. A few allow the programmer to refer to A(0), but this is the exception rather than the rule.

6. Subscripts must be positive integers or integer expressions. If you must use a real expression to compute the value of a subscript, use the INT predefined function to convert it to integer form.

7. Avoid "out-of-bounds" subscripts. For example, the element X(15) does not exist in a ten-element array, nor does X(-1). Most versions of FORTRAN will terminate your program when such conditions are encountered. A few do not, generating unpredictable results. If there is a chance that a subscript will go out-of-bounds as a result of bad input data or a computation, test the subscript before using it.

8. A few versions of FORTRAN initialize the value of each element in an array, usually to zero. Most do not. Don't assume anything. Even if your system initial-

158

izes an array, code the instructions to provide initial values. It is simply bad coding practice to rely on assumed defaults.

9. A few versions of FORTRAN will assume the size of an array if you fail to code a DIMENSION statement. Once again, don't rely on the default—code the DIMENSION statement.

10. Occasionally, you will encounter a need to code an array without knowing how many elements will be present. You will be tempted to code something like:

DIMENSION   X(N)   *Note: illegal.*

Don't. It's illegal. In most versions of FORTRAN, you *must* specify the number of elements in the array. The only exception is in a subroutine, a subject we shall return to shortly.

CHARACTER ARRAYS

A character array is defined in a CHARACTER statement or in a DIMENSION statement following a CHARACTER statement. For example, the statement:

CHARACTER*15   NAME(25)

defines an array of twenty-five 15-character elements. The same array could have been defined by coding:

CHARACTER*15   NAME

DIMENSION   NAME(25)

Note that the type statement must come first.

An array of twenty asterisks might be defined by coding:

CHARACTER*1   ASTER(20)

Space to hold one hundred 10-character city names could be defined by coding:

CHARACTER*10   CITY(100)

Note that the number of characters *in each element* immediately follows the "CHARACTER*", while the number of elements in the array is enclosed in parentheses after the array name.

1. Imagine that your instructor has decided to use the computer to keep track of your course grades for the current term. For each student in the class, the following information is to be stored: identification number, name, first exam grade, second exam grade, third exam grade, final exam grade, and homework grade. One array is to be set up for each data item. Write the code needed to initialize each array. How many elements will be in each array? Which arrays will be character and which numeric? Can you possibly initialize all elements in all arrays now? Set any field that is unknown at the beginning of the term to zero.

MULTI-DIMENSIONAL ARRAYS

FORTRAN supports arrays with as many as seven dimensions (usually). For example, the statement:

DIMENSION(5,5)

would create an array of 5 rows and 5 columns; a representation of this array is shown as Fig. D.1. Note that there are 25 elements in the array; each of the 5 rows contains 5 columns. Each element in the array is defined by two subscripts; for example, the element at the top left is A(1,1), while the one in the middle of the array is A(3,3). Any number of rows and columns may be coded (up to the limit imposed by your system, of course). For example, the statement:

DIMENSION(2,4)

would define an array of eight elements.

Fig. D.1: *A two-dimensional array.*

A(1,1)	A(1,2)	A(1,3)	A(1,4)	A(1,5)
A(2,1)	A(2,2)	A(2,3)	A(2,4)	A(2,5)
A(3,1)	A(3,2)	A(3,3)	A(3,4)	A(3,5)
A(4,1)	A(4,2)	A(4,3)	A(4,4)	A(4,5)
A(5,1)	A(5,2)	A(5,3)	A(5,4)	A(5,5)

A three-dimensional array is one that has three subscripts. For example, the statement:

DIMENSION   R(2,3,4)

would create a "2 by 3 by 4" array, giving a total of 24 elements. The rules for coding subscripts are the same as they were with single-dimensional arrays. By controlling subscript values, the programmer can manipulate the individual elements of a multi-dimensional array.

A very common application for 2-dimensional arrays is linear algebra, a mathematical tool that is used in solving a number of operations research or management science problems. Business programmers will often code tax tables and similar tables as array structures. This text will stop with arrays of one dimension. If you continue with your computer-related studies, however, you will almost certainly encounter a need for arrays of more dimensions.

PASSING ARRAYS TO A SUBROUTINE

An array can be passed to (or from) a subroutine. Simply include the array name in the list following the CALL statement, and indicate an array name in the same relative position in the list following the subroutine statement. The array types must match; you cannot, for example, pass an integer array to a real array.

You *must* identify the array *within* the subroutine with a DIMENSION statement (or explicit type statement). This can be done by explicitly declaring the array size; for example:

SUBROUTINE   NAME   (X,Y)

DIMENSION   X(50),Y(50)

Since the array is defined in the main program, and not (usually) in the subroutine, the subroutine often does not care how big the array actually is. Thus, in many versions of FORTRAN, the programmer is allowed to define an array of unspecified dimension; for example:

SUBROUTINE   NAME   (X,Y)

DIMENSION   X(*),Y(*)

The actual number of elements will be controlled by the main program. Note that the array type (integer, real) and the number of subscripts (3-dimensions, 4-dimensions) must match. The *only* time an array can be defined without specifying the number of elements is within a subroutine; if you try it within your main program, it won't work.

What Next? 7

This is a book on the FORTRAN language. The title is *FORTRAN 77: Getting Started*. The title very clearly describes the book's intent: to help you get started as a programmer.

Assuming that you have read carefully, assuming (more importantly) that you have written a number of programs, you now know how to program. You have learned a valuable skill. As is the case with any skill, however, "practice makes perfect". You are still a novice. The only way to *really* learn how to program *is* to program. No matter what your field of major study, no matter what your job may be, computer programming can be an invaluable tool. But it's all up to you. If you use your skill, you will get better. If you choose not to use it, you will probably lose it.

As you begin to write more and more significant programs, you will eventually have a need for features of the FORTRAN language that were not covered here. Where do you find information on these features? In a reference manual; you should be able to find a copy somewhere in or near your computer center. Reference manuals are not written for beginners; they are written for people who already know how to program. Reference manuals describe, in detail, precisely how specific instructions work. If you cannot figure out what instruction should be coded next, the reference manual will not help you; if you *know* what instruction should be coded next, the reference manual will show you how to code it. You know how to program. You can read the reference manual. Learn to use it. Of course, there are other sources of programming information—other programmers. Ask. Most programmers are only too happy to show a novice a few tricks.

But the bottom line remains: The only way to learn to program *is* to program. Do it. That's how you will learn.

SOME POINTERS

There are a few FORTRAN features that you will almost certainly encounter as your skill increases. Consider, for example, data type. We worked with integers, real numbers, and character fields in this text. Double precision and complex numbers are also available. Look them up.

FORMAT statements is another topic that we just "touched on". There are dozens of different types of FORMAT statements. We have covered the most commonly used FORMAT items. You may have already sensed that some of our output left a bit to be desired. Perhaps a few more advanced FORMAT statements were just what we needed.

In module D, we briefly mentioned multi-dimensional arrays. As your skills in both programming and mathematics improve, you may well want to use multi-dimensional arrays.

One of the real advantages of the FORTRAN language is the tremendous collection of scientific subroutines that are available through this language. If you ever come across a complex scientific computation, the chances are that someone else has already written a FORTRAN subroutine to solve it. By simply writing a skeleton FORTRAN program that provides input data, CALLs the subroutine, and prints the results, you can tap this vast treasure of computational aids. Virtually any statistical technique you might care to mention is available, along with most of the commonly used management science or operations research models. Ask your instructor what is available on your system.

A few other statements you may need are the DATA statement, the EQUIVALENCE declaration, and the COMMON statement. Look them up. More advanced programming often requires the use of magnetic disk or magnetic tape as an input or output device. FORTRAN supports such I/O devices; look in your reference manual to find out how.

It's up to you.

Answers to
Selected Exercises

MODULE A, page 47.

1. a. correct. integer.
   b. correct. real.
   c. correct. real. Note that the blank may cause problems.
   d. incorrect. comma is illegal.
   e. incorrect. real. Too many digits; will be stored as 123456.7.
   f. correct. real.
   g. correct. integer.
   h. correct. integer.
   i. correct. real.
   j. correct. integer. Close to upper limit.
   k. correct. real.
   l. correct. real.

2. a. 3.14159
   b. 0.3937 inches/centimeter or 2.54 centimeters/inch.
   c. 39.37 inches/meter.
   d. 0.6214 miles/kilometer or 1.6093 kilometers/mile.
   e. 4.000.
   f. Varies. Typically, about 64 semester hours for an associate degree and 128 for a bachelor's degree.
   g. 225.0E6 or about 225 million.
   h. 1.0E−8. Roughly one angstrom unit.
   i. Alpha Centari is 4.3 light years away.
   j. 5.8657E12 miles/light year.
   k. A typical FM station would be 100 megahertz or 100E6 hertz. A typical AM station would be 700 kilohertz or 700E3 hertz.
   l. Probably something like 5.25. Why have we not coded a dollar sign?
   m. About 6000.00.
   n. 33.33333.

MODULE A, page 49.

1. a. integer.   g. real
   b. illegal. Too many characters.   h. integer
   c. real.   i. integer.

d.	real.	j.	illegal. Too many characters.
e.	real.	k.	integer.
f.	real.	l.	integer.

2. You may, of course, have selected different variable names. Note carefully the data type.

a.	PI	h.	ATOM.
b.	CENTI	i.	STAR
c.	CMETER	j.	YEAR
d.	CKILO	k.	HERTZ
e.	GPA	l.	RATE
f.	CREDIT	m.	PRICE
g.	POPUS	n.	RPM

MODULE A, page 53.

1. a. X + Y + (2.0 * Z) + 8.0   Note: parentheses not necessary.
   b. (2.0 * A) + (4.0 * B) + (4.0 * C) – (2.0 * D)   Note: parentheses not necessary.
   c. (X + Y) / (A + B)
   d. ((-B) + ((B ** 2 – 4.0 * A * C) ** 0.5)) / (2.0 * A)
   e. (X * Y) – (2.0 * (X ** 2) * (Y ** 2)) + (3.0 * (X ** 3) * (Y ** 3))
   f. (A / 3.0) + ((B ** 2) / 4.0) – ((C ** 3) / 3.0)
   g. ((A * B * C * D) / (W * X * Y * Z)) + 18.5

2. a. 0.5 * BASE * HEIGHT
   b. SIDE ** 3
   c. 3.1416 * (RADIUS ** 3)
   d. 3.1416 * (RADIUS ** 2) * HEIGHT
   e. HITS / ATBAT
   f. RUNS / (INNS / 9.0)
   g. GDPTS / CREDIT
   h. OLDBAL * 0.05

3. a. 4.5
   b. The answer is 4.   Note: 2/4=0 in integer.
   c. 7.5
   d. 2
   e. 12.0
   f. 12
   g. 36.0
   h. The answer is 4.   Note: 3/2=1 in integer.
   i. 4.5
   j. The answer is 0.   Note: 3/4=0 in integer.

MOUDLE B, page 87.

1. a. I2
   b. F4.3 or F5.3 for output.
   c. I9 or E7.1
   d. F8.5
   e. I2

2. FORMAT   (I8,T11,F4.2,T21,F3.1,T31,I3)
   or: FORMAT   (I8,2X,F4.2,6X,F3.1,7X,I3)

3. FORMAT   (T10,'NUMBER',T20,'SQUARE ROOT')
   FORMAT   (T12,I3,T22,F7.4)

4. FORMAT   ('1',T10,'CUSTOMER',T25,'OLD BALANCE',T40,'CHECKS',
              T55,'DEPOSITS',T70,'NEW BALANCE')
   FORMAT   (T10,I8,T25,F10.2,T40,F10.2,T55,F10.2,T69,F11.2)

FORTRAN Instruction Quick Reference

Use the following index to quickly find the page where a given FORTRAN instruction is explained.